Coaching
Youth Wrestling

Second Edition

American Sport Education Program

Human Kinetics

Library of Congress Cataloging-in-Publication Data

Coaching youth wrestling / American Sport Education Program. -- 2nd ed.
    p. cm.
    ISBN 0-7360-4159-1
        1. Wrestling for children--Coaching--United States--Handbooks, manuals, etc. I.
    American Sport Education Program.
    GV1196.3 .C63 2001
    797.812--dc21

                                                              2001039617

ISBN: 0-7360-4159-1

Materials in chapters 4 and 6 are reprinted, by permission, from the YMCA of the USA, 1999, *YMCA Coaching Winners Baseball and Softball*. (Champaign, IL: Human Kinetics).

Consultants: Ed McNeely, Ted Witalski; **Acquisitions Editor**: Karen Decker; **Managing Editor**: Wendy McLaughlin; **Assistant Editor**: Dan Brachtesende; **Copyeditor**: Patsy Fortney; **Proofreader**: Joanna Hatzopolous Portman; **Permission Manager:** Toni Harte; **Graphic Designer**: Fred Starbird; **Graphic Artist**: Francine Hamerski; **Photo Manager**: Les Woodrum; **Cover Designer**: Jack W. Davis; **Photographer (cover)**: Eric Berndt; **Photographer (interior)**: Les Woodrum; **Printer**: United Graphics

Copies of this book are available at special discounts for bulk purchase for sales promotions, premiums, fund-raising, or educational use. Special editions or book excerpts can also be created to specifications. For details, contact the Special Sales Manager at Human Kinetics.

Printed in the United States of America   10 9 8 7 6 5 4 3

Human Kinetics
Web site: www.HumanKinetics.com

United States: Human Kinetics, P.O. Box 5076, Champaign, IL 61825-5076
800-747-4457
e-mail: humank@hkusa.com

Canada: Human Kinetics, 475 Devonshire Road, Unit 100, Windsor, ON N8Y 2L5
800-465-7301 (in Canada only)
e-mail: orders@hkcanada.com

Europe: Human Kinetics, 107 Bradford Road, Stanningley
Leeds LS28 6AT, United Kingdom
+44 (0) 113 255 5665
e-mail: hk@hkeurope.com

Australia: Human Kinetics, 57A Price Avenue, Lower Mitcham, South Australia 5062
08 8277 1555
e-mail: liahka@senet.com.au

New Zealand: Human Kinetics, P.O. Box 105-231, Auckland Central
09-523-3462
e-mail: hkp@ihug.co.nz

Coaching
Youth Wrestling

Contents

Welcome to Coaching!

Coaching young people is an exciting way to be involved in sports. But it isn't easy. Some coaches are overwhelmed by the responsibilities involved in helping athletes through their early sport experiences. That's not surprising because coaching youngsters requires more than telling them to lace up their shoes and step on the mat. It involves preparing them physically and mentally to compete effectively, fairly, and safely in their sport, while providing them with a positive role model.

This book will help you meet those challenges and experience the many rewards of coaching young athletes. You'll learn how to meet your responsibilities as a coach, communicate well and provide for safety, use a highly effective method—the games approach—to teaching tactics and skills, and coach effectively on match day. We also provide three sets of season plans to guide you throughout your season.

This book serves as a text for ASEP's Coaching Youth Sport course. If you would like more information about this course or other ASEP courses and resources, please contact us at

ASEP
P.O. Box 5076
Champaign, IL 61825-5076
1-800-747-5698
www.asep.com

Foreword

Whether you are a volunteer club coach or a scholastic coach with a little experience, you already know that youngsters are not mature adults. Young people have different perspectives, experience different emotions, and set different goals than older people do. They present special challenges to a coach because they react differently than adults to instruction, criticism, encouragement, failure, and success. This book will help you meet those challenges and experience the rewards of coaching young athletes. It is intended for adults with little or no formal preparation to coach wrestlers.

Coaching Youth Wrestling is the result of a joint effort by USA Wrestling and the American Sport Education Program (ASEP). The book serves as the Copper Introductory Level text in USA Wrestling's National Coaches Education Program (NCEP). It is the first resource wrestling coaches need to advance to Bronze Leader, Silver Achiever, and Gold Master levels in the NCEP.

USA Wrestling and ASEP hope you will find coaching rewarding and will continue to learn more about coaching and the sport of wrestling so that you can be the best possible coach for your athletes. Good coaching!

For more information about this coaching education program, please contact:

USA Wrestling
National Coaches Education Program
6155 Lehman Drive
Colorado Springs, CO 80918
719-598-8181

chapter 1

Stepping Into Coaching

If you are like most youth wrestling coaches, you have probably been recruited from the ranks of concerned parents, sport enthusiasts, or community volunteers. Like many rookie and veteran coaches, you probably have had little formal instruction on how to coach. But when the call went out for coaches to assist with the local youth wrestling program, you answered because you like children and enjoy wrestling, and perhaps because you wanted to be involved in a worthwhile community activity.

Your initial coaching assignment may be difficult. Like many volunteers, you may not know everything there is to know about wrestling or about how to work with children. *Coaching Youth Wrestling* will help you learn the basics of coaching wrestling effectively.

To start, let's take a look at what's involved in being a coach. We'll discuss your responsibilities and how to handle having your own child on the team you coach. We'll also examine five tools for being an effective coach.

Your Responsibilities As a Coach

As a wrestling coach, you'll be called on to do the following:

1. **Provide a safe physical environment.** Wrestling holds an inherent risk, but as a coach you're responsible for regularly inspecting the practice and competition areas. (See the checklists for facilities and equipment in chapter 6.)

2. **Communicate in a positive way.** Because you'll be communicating not only with your athletes but also with parents, officials, and administrators, you'll want to do so in a way that is positive and that demonstrates you have the best interests of the athletes at heart. Chapter 2 will offer tips on how to communicate effectively and positively.

3. **Teach the skills of wrestling.** In chapter 4 we'll introduce you to an innovative "games approach" to teaching and practicing the skills young athletes need to know—an approach that kids thoroughly enjoy. This approach will help you meet the goal of helping all athletes be the best they can be. In chapter 5 we'll show you how to teach wrestling skills, and in chapter 10 we'll provide season plans for children ages 9 and under, 10 and 11, and 12 and over, respectively. In chapter 9 we'll provide descriptions of all the skills you'll need to teach and help you detect and correct errors that athletes typically make.

4. **Teach the rules of wrestling.** You'll find the rules of wrestling that you'll need to teach your athletes in chapter 7.

5. **Direct athletes in competition.** This includes selecting players in each weight group, relating appropriately to officials and to opposing coaches and athletes, and making tactical decisions during matches. (See chapter 6.) Remember that the focus is not on winning at all costs, but on coaching your kids to compete well, do their best, and strive to win within the rules.

6. **Help your athletes become fit and value fitness for a lifetime.** You will want to help your athletes be fit so that they can wrestle safely and successfully, but you'll also want them to learn to become fit on their own, understand the value of fitness, and enjoy training. Thus, it is best not to make them do push-ups or run laps as punishment. Make it fun to get fit for wrestling, and make it fun to wrestle so that they'll stay fit. Chapter 8 illustrates conditioning and diet regimens appropriate for young wrestlers.

7. **Help young people develop character.** Character development includes learning caring, honesty, respect, and responsibility. These intangible qualities are no less important to teach than the skill of a good cradle for the pin. You can teach these values to athletes both by conducting team circles after every match and by demonstrating and encouraging behaviors that express these values at all times.

These are your responsibilities as a coach. But coaching becomes even more complicated when your child is in the club or team you coach. If this is the case, you'll have to take into account your roles as both a coach and a parent, and think about how those roles relate to each other.

Coaching Your Own Child

Many coaches are parents, but the two roles should not be confused. Unlike your role as a parent, as a coach you are responsible not only to yourself and your child, but also to the organization, all the athletes on the team (including your child), and their parents. Because of this additional responsibility, your behavior on the wrestling mat will be different from your behavior at home, and your child may not understand why.

For example, imagine the confusion of a young boy who is the center of his parents' attention at home but is barely noticed by his father/coach in the sport setting. You need to explain to your son your new responsibilities and how they will affect your relationship when coaching.

Take the following steps to avoid problems when coaching your child:

- Ask your child if he wants you to coach the team.
- Explain why you wish to be involved with the team.
- Discuss with your child how your interactions will change when you take on the role of coach at practices or games.
- Limit your coaching behavior to when you are in the coaching role.
- Avoid parenting during practice or game situations, to keep your role clear in your child's mind.
- Reaffirm your love for your child, irrespective of his performance on the wrestling mat.

Now let's look at some of the qualities that will help you become an effective coach.

Five Tools of an Effective Coach

Have you purchased the traditional coaching tools—things like whistles, coaching clothes, wrestling shoes, and a clipboard? They'll help you coach, but to be a successful coach you'll need five other tools that cannot be bought. These tools are available only through self-examination and hard work; they're easy to remember with the acronym COACH:

C – Comprehension

O – Outlook

A – Affection

C – Character

H – Humor

Comprehension

Comprehension of the rules and skills of wrestling is required. You must understand the basic elements of the sport. To assist you in learning about the game, we describe rules and skills in chapters 7 and 9. We also provide season plans in chapter 10.

To improve your comprehension of wrestling, take the following steps:

- Read the sport-specific section of this book in chapters 7, 8, and 9.
- Consider reading other wrestling coaching books, including those available from the American Sport Education Program (ASEP).
- Contact USA Wrestling or visit TheMat.com at www.themat.com.
- Attend wrestling clinics.
- Talk with more experienced coaches.
- Observe local college, high school, and youth wrestling.
- Watch wrestling on television or order videotapes of matches.

In addition to having wrestling knowledge, you must implement proper training and safety methods so your athletes can participate with little risk of injury. Even then, injuries may occur. More often than not, you'll be the first person responding to your athletes' injuries, so be sure you understand the basic emergency care procedures described in chapter 3. Also, read in that chapter how to handle more serious sport injury situations.

Outlook

This coaching tool refers to your perspective and goals—what you are seeking as a coach. The most common coaching objectives are to (1) have fun; (2) help athletes develop their physical, mental, and social skills; and (3) win. Thus your outlook involves the priorities you set, your planning, and your vision for the future.

While all coaches focus on competition, we believe it is best to focus on positive competition, keeping the pursuit of victory in perspective by making decisions that first are in the best interest of the athletes, and second will help those athletes win.

So how do you know if your outlook and priorities are in order? Here's a little test for you:

Which of the following situations would you be most proud of?

a. Knowing that each participant enjoyed wrestling

b. Seeing that all athletes improved their wrestling skills

c. Winning the league championship

Which of the following statements best reflects your thoughts about sport?

a. If it isn't fun, don't do it.

b. Everyone should learn something every day.

c. Wrestling isn't fun if you don't win.

How would you like your athletes to remember you?

a. As a coach who was fun to wrestle for

b. As a coach who provided a good base of fundamental skills

c. As a coach who had a winning record

Which of the following statements would you most like to hear a parent of an athlete on your team say?

a. Mike really had a good time wrestling this year.

b. George learned some important lessons wrestling this year.

c. Willie was on the championship wrestling team this year.

Which of the following would be the most rewarding moment of your season?

   a. Having your team not want to stop wrestling, even after practice is over

   b. Seeing one of your athletes finally master the skill of a difficult upper-body throw

   c. Winning the league championship

Look over your answers. If you most often selected "a" responses, then having fun is most important to you. A majority of "b" answers suggests that skill development is what attracts you to coaching. And if "c" was your most frequent response, winning is tops on your list of coaching priorities. If your priorities are in order, your athletes' well-being will take precedence over your team's win–loss record every time.

The American Sport Education Program (ASEP) has a motto that will help you keep your outlook in line with the best interests of the kids on your team. It summarizes in four words all you need to remember when establishing your coaching priorities:

Athletes First, Winning Second

This motto recognizes that striving to win is an important, even vital, part of sports. But it emphatically states that no efforts in striving to win should be made at the expense of the athletes' well-being, development, and enjoyment.

Take the following actions to better define your outlook:

1. Determine your priorities for the season.
2. Prepare for situations that challenge your priorities.
3. Set goals for yourself and your athletes that are consistent with those priorities.
4. Plan how you and your athletes can best attain those goals.
5. Review your goals frequently to be sure that you are staying on track.

Affection

Another vital tool you will want to have in your coaching kit is a genuine concern for the young people you coach. It involves having a love for kids, a desire to share with them your love and knowledge of wrestling, and the patience and understanding that allow each individual playing for you to grow from his or her involvement in sport. You can demonstrate your affection and patience in many ways, including these:

⊚ Make an effort to get to know each athlete on your team.

⊚ Treat each athlete as an individual.

⊚ Empathize with athletes trying to learn new and difficult skills.

⊚ Treat athletes as you would like to be treated under similar circumstances.

⊚ Be in control of your emotions.

⊚ Show your enthusiasm for being involved with your team.

⊚ Keep an upbeat and positive tone in all of your communications.

Character

The fact that you have decided to coach young wrestlers probably means that you think participation in sport is important. But whether or not that participation develops character in your athletes depends as much on you as it does on the sport itself. How can you build character in your athletes?

Having good character means behaving appropriately in sport and life. Encouraging such behavior in your athletes requires more than just saying the right things. What you say and what you do must match. There is no place in coaching for the "Do as I say, not as I do" philosophy. If you challenge, support, encourage, and reward every youngster, your athletes will be more likely to accept, even celebrate, their differences. Be in control before, during, and after all practices and contests. And don't be afraid to admit that you were wrong. No one is perfect!

Consider the following steps to being a good role model:

⊚ Take stock of your strengths and weaknesses.

⊚ Build on your strengths.

⊚ Set goals for yourself to improve those areas you would not like to see copied.

⊚ If you slip up, apologize to your team and to yourself. You'll do better next time.

Humor

Humor is an often-overlooked coaching tool. For our use it means having the ability to laugh at yourself and with your athletes during practices and contests. Nothing helps balance the tone of a serious skill-learning session like a chuckle or two. Also, a sense of humor puts in perspective the many mistakes your athletes will make. Try not to get upset over each miscue or respond negatively to erring athletes. Allow your athletes and yourself to enjoy the ups, and don't dwell on the downs.

Here are some tips for injecting humor into your practices:

- Make practices fun by including a variety of activities.
- Keep all athletes involved in games and skill practices.
- Consider laughter by your athletes a sign of enjoyment, not of waning discipline.
- Smile!

Communicating
As a Coach

In chapter 1 you learned about the tools needed to COACH: Comprehension, Outlook, Affection, Character, and Humor. These are essentials for effective coaching; without them, you'll have a difficult time getting started. But none of the tools will work if you don't know how to use them with your athletes—and this requires skillful communication. This chapter examines what communication is and how you can become a more effective communicator-coach.

What's Involved in Communication?

Coaches often mistakenly believe that communication involves only instructing athletes to do something, but verbal commands are only a small part of the communication process. More than half of what is communicated is nonverbal. So remember when you are coaching: Actions speak louder than words.

Communication in its simplest form involves two people: a sender and a receiver. The sender transmits the message verbally, through facial expressions, and possibly through body language. Once the message is sent, the receiver must assimilate it successfully. A receiver who fails to attend or listen will miss parts, if not all, of the message.

Sending More Effective Messages

Young athletes often have little understanding of the rules and skills of wrestling and probably even less confidence in their ability to wrestle. For these reasons, they need accurate, understandable, and supportive messages to help them along. That's why your verbal and nonverbal messages are so important.

Verbal Messages

"Sticks and stones may break my bones, but words will never hurt me" isn't true. Spoken words can have a strong and long-lasting effect. Coaches' words are particularly influential because youngsters place great importance on what coaches say. Perhaps you, like many former youth sport participants, have a difficult time remembering much of anything you were told by your elementary school teachers, but you can still recall several specific things your coaches at that level said to you. Such is the lasting effect of a coach's comments to an athlete.

Whether you are correcting misbehavior, teaching an athlete how to counter a double-leg, or praising an athlete for good effort, you should consider a number of things when sending a message verbally, including the following:

- Be positive and honest.
- Speak clearly and simply.
- Speak loudly enough and repeat what you say.
- Be consistent.

Be Positive and Honest

Nothing turns people off like hearing someone nag all the time, and athletes react similarly to a coach who gripes constantly. Young athletes particularly need encouragement because they often doubt their ability to perform in a sport. So look for and tell your athletes what they did well.

But don't cover up poor or incorrect wrestling with rosy words of praise. Kids know all too well when they've erred, and no cheerfully expressed cliché can undo their mistakes. If you fail to acknowledge athletes' errors, your athletes will think you are a phony.

A good way to correct a performance error is first to point out what the athlete did correctly. Then explain in a positive way what he or she is doing wrong and show him or her how to correct it. Finish by encouraging the athlete and emphasizing the correct performance.

Be sure not to follow a positive statement with the word *but*. For example, don't say, "Nice shot, but if you would keep your elbows in, you'd get the takedown." Saying it this way causes many kids to ignore the positive statement and focus on the negative one. Instead, say something like, "That was a good setup for your shot, Chris. And if you keep your elbows tighter to your body, you'll get that takedown next time. That was right on target. That's the way to go."

Speak Clearly and Simply

Positive and honest messages are good, but only if expressed directly in words your athletes understand. Beating around the bush is ineffective and inefficient. If you ramble, your athletes will miss the point of your message and probably lose interest. Here are some tips for saying things clearly:

⊙ Organize your thoughts before speaking to your athletes.

⊙ Explain things thoroughly, but don't bore them with long-winded monologues.

⊙ Use language your athletes can understand. However, avoid trying to be hip by using their age group's slang vocabulary.

Speak Loudly Enough, and Repeat What You Say

Talk to your team in a voice that all members can hear and interpret. A crisp, vigorous voice commands attention and respect; garbled and weak speech is tuned out. It's OK—in fact, appropriate—to soften your voice when speaking to an athlete individually about a personal problem.

But most of the time your messages will be for all your athletes to hear, so make sure they can! An enthusiastic voice also motivates athletes and tells them you enjoy being their coach. A word of caution, however: Don't dominate the setting with a booming voice that diverts attention from athletes' performances.

Sometimes what you say, even if stated loudly and clearly, won't sink in the first time. This may be particularly true when young athletes hear words they don't understand. To avoid boring repetition and yet still get your message across, say the same thing in a slightly different way. For instance, you might first tell your athletes, "Remember to keep your feet wide when you're in your stance." If they don't appear to understand, you might say, "When you're wrestling on your feet, if you keep your feet spread apart, you'll be better able to defend against your opponent's attacks." The second form of the message may get through to athletes who missed it the first time around.

Be Consistent

People often say things in ways that imply a different message. For example, a touch of sarcasm added to the words "Way to go!" sends an entirely different message than the words themselves suggest. Avoid sending such mixed messages. Keep the tone of your voice consistent with the words you use. And don't say something one day and contradict it the next; athletes will get their wires crossed.

Nonverbal Messages

Just as you should be consistent in the tone of voice and words you use, you should also keep your verbal and nonverbal messages consistent. An extreme example of failing to do this would be shaking your head, indicating disapproval, while at the same time telling an athlete "Nice try." Which is the athlete to believe, your gesture or your words?

Messages can be sent nonverbally in a number of ways. Facial expressions and body language are just two of the more obvious forms of nonverbal signals that can help you when you coach.

Facial Expressions

The look on a person's face is the quickest clue to what he thinks or feels. Your athletes know this, so they will study your face, looking for any sign that will tell them more than the words you say. Don't try to fool them by putting on a happy or blank "mask." They'll see through it, and you'll lose credibility.

Serious, stone-faced expressions are no help to kids who need cues as to how they are performing. They will just assume you're unhappy or disinterested. Don't be afraid to smile. A smile from a coach can give a great boost to an unsure athlete. Plus, a smile lets your athletes know that you are happy coaching them. But don't overdo it, or your athletes won't be able to tell whether you are genuinely pleased by something they've done or are just putting on a smiling face.

Body Language

What would your athletes think you were feeling if you came to practice slouched over, with your head down and shoulders slumped? Tired? Bored? Unhappy? What would they think you were feeling if you watched them during a contest with your hands on your hips, your jaws clenched, and your face reddened? Upset with them? Disgusted with an official? Mad at a fan? Probably some or all of these things would enter your athletes' minds. None of these impressions is the kind you want your athletes to have of you. That's why you should carry yourself in a pleasant, confident, and vigorous manner. Such a posture not only projects happiness with your coaching role but also provides a good example for your young athletes, who may model your behavior.

Physical contact can also be a very important use of body language. A handshake, a pat on the head, an arm around the shoulder, or even a big hug are effective ways of showing approval, concern, affection, and joy to your athletes. Youngsters are especially in need of this type of nonverbal message. Keep within the obvious moral and legal limits, of course, but don't be reluctant to touch your athletes, sending a message that can only truly be expressed in that way.

Improving Receiving Skills

Now, let's examine the other half of the communication process—receiving messages. Too often very good message senders are very poor message receivers. As a coach of young athletes, you must be able to fulfill both roles effectively.

The requirements for receiving messages are quite simple, but receiving skills are perhaps less satisfying and therefore underdeveloped compared to sending skills. People seem to naturally enjoy hearing themselves talk more than hearing others talk. But if you read about the keys to receiving messages and make a strong effort to use them with your athletes, you'll be surprised by what you've been missing.

Attention!

First, you must pay attention; you must want to hear what others have to communicate to you. That's not always easy when you're busy coaching and have many things competing for your attention. But in one-on-one or team meetings with athletes, you must really focus on what they are telling you, both verbally and nonverbally. You'll be amazed at the little signals you pick up. Not only will such focused attention help you catch every word your athletes say, but also you'll notice your athletes' moods and physical states. In addition, you'll get an idea of your athletes' feelings toward you and other athletes on the team.

Listen *CARE-FULLY*

How we receive messages from others, perhaps more than anything else we do, demonstrates how much we care for the sender and what that person has to tell us. If you care little for your athletes or have little regard for what they have to say, it will show in how you attend and listen to them. Check yourself. Do you find your mind wandering to what you are going to do after practice while one of your athletes is talking to you? Do you frequently have to ask your athletes, "What did you say?" If so, you need to work on your receiving mechanics of attending and listening. But perhaps the most critical question you should ask yourself, if you find that you're missing the messages your athletes send, is this: Do I care?

Providing Feedback

So far we've discussed separately the sending and receiving of messages. But we all know that senders and receivers switch roles several times during an interaction. One person initiates a communication by sending a message to another person, who then receives the message. The receiver then switches roles and becomes the sender by responding to the person who sent the initial message. These verbal and nonverbal responses are called feedback.

Your athletes will be looking to you for feedback all the time. They will want to know how you think they are performing, what you think of their ideas, and whether their efforts please you. Obviously, you can respond in many different ways. How you respond will strongly affect your athletes. They will respond most favorably to positive feedback.

Praising athletes when they have performed or behaved well is an effective way of getting them to repeat (or try to repeat) that behavior in the future. In addition, positive feedback for effort is an especially effective way to motivate youngsters to work on difficult skills. So rather than shouting and providing negative feedback to athletes who have made mistakes, try offering athletes positive feedback, letting them know what they did correctly and how they can improve.

Sometimes just the way you word feedback can make it more positive than negative. For example, instead of saying, "Don't shoot from so far away," you might say, "Get closer before you attack." Then your athletes will be focusing on what to do instead of what not to do.

You can give positive feedback verbally and nonverbally. Telling an athlete, especially in front of teammates, that he has performed well is a great way to boost the confidence of a youngster. A pat on the back or a handshake can be a very tangible way of communicating your recognition of an athlete's performance.

Communicating With Others in the Wrestling Community

Coaching involves not only sending and receiving messages and providing proper feedback to athletes, but also interacting with parents, fans, game officials, and opposing coaches. If you don't communicate effectively with these groups of people, your coaching career will be unpleasant and short-lived. So try the following suggestions for communicating with these groups.

Parents

An athlete's parents need to be assured that their child is under the direction of a coach who is both knowledgeable about the sport and concerned about the youngster's well-being. You can put their worries to rest by holding a preseason parent-orientation meeting in which you describe your background and your approach to coaching.

If parents contact you with a concern during the season, listen to them closely and try to offer positive responses. If you need to communicate with parents, catch them after a practice, give them a phone call, or send a note through the mail. Messages sent to parents through athletes are too often lost, misinterpreted, or forgotten.

Fans

The stands probably won't be overflowing at your matches, but that only means that you'll more easily hear the few fans who criticize your coaching. When you hear something negative about the job you're doing, don't respond. Keep calm, consider whether the message had any value, and if not, forget it. Acknowledging critical, unwarranted comments from a fan during a match will only encourage others to voice their opinions. So put away your "rabbit ears" and communicate to fans, through your actions, that you are a confident, competent coach.

Prepare your athletes for fans' criticisms. Tell them it is you, not the spectators, they should listen to. If you notice that one of your athletes is rattled by a fan's comment, reassure the athlete that your evaluation is more objective and favorable—and the one that counts.

Match Officials

How you communicate with officials will have a great influence on the way your athletes behave toward them. Therefore, you need to set an example. Greet officials with a handshake, an introduction, and perhaps some casual conversation about the upcoming match. Indicate your respect for them before, during, and after the match. Don't make nasty remarks, shout, or use disrespectful body gestures. Your athletes will see you do it, and they'll get the idea that such behavior is appropriate. Plus, if the official hears or sees you, the communication between the two of you will break down.

Opposing Coaches

Make an effort to visit with the coach of the opposing team before the match. During the match, don't get into a personal feud with the opposing coach. Remember, it's the kids, not the coaches, who are competing. By getting along well with the opposing coach, you'll show your athletes that competition involves cooperation.

Providing for Athletes' Safety

As they are reviewing single-leg setups and finishes, Jason begins to work through takedowns with Bryan, giving him a good
look of resistance. Jason tree-tops Bryan to the mat, and at first
everything seems to be normal. However, Bryan gets up slowly and
obviously has pain in his shoulder. You ask Bryan to come over,
and you quickly see he has an injury, maybe a collar-bone fracture.
What do you do?

No coach wants to see athletes get hurt. But injury remains a reality of
sport participation; consequently, you must be prepared to provide first
aid when injuries occur and to protect yourself against unjustified lawsuits. Fortunately, there are many preventive measures coaches can institute to reduce the risk. In this chapter we describe steps you can take
to prevent injuries, first aid and emergency responses for when injuries
occur, and your legal responsibilities as a coach.

Game Plan for Safety

You can't prevent all injuries from happening, but you can take preventive measures that give your athletes the best possible chance for injury-free participation. To help you create the safest possible environment for your athletes, we'll explore what you can do in these six areas:

⊙ Preseason physical examinations
⊙ Physical conditioning
⊙ Equipment and facilities inspection
⊙ Athlete matchups and inherent risks
⊙ Proper supervision and record keeping
⊙ Environmental conditions

We'll begin with what should take place before the season begins: the preseason physical examination.

Preseason Physical Examination

We recommend that your athletes have a physical examination before participating in wrestling. The exam should address the most likely areas of medical concern and identify youngsters at high risk. We also suggest that you have athletes' parents or guardians sign a participation agreement form and a release form to allow their children to be treated in case of an emergency.

Physical Conditioning

Athletes need to be in, or get in, shape to wrestle at the expected level. To do so, they'll need to have adequate cardiorespiratory fitness and muscular fitness.

Cardiorespiratory fitness involves the body's ability to store and use oxygen and fuels efficiently to power muscle contractions. As athletes get in better shape, their bodies are able to more efficiently deliver oxygen and fuels to muscles and carry off carbon dioxides and other wastes. Wrestling involves lots of movement and requires short bursts of energy throughout a match.

An advantage of teaching wrestling with the games approach is that kids are active during almost the entire practice; there is no standing around in lines watching teammates take part in drills. Athletes will be attaining higher levels of cardiorespiratory fitness as the season progresses simply by taking part in practice. However, watch closely for signs of low levels of cardiorespiratory fitness; don't let your athletes do too much until they're fit. You might privately counsel youngsters who appear overly winded, suggesting that they train outside of practice to increase their fitness.

Muscular fitness encompasses strength, muscle endurance, power, speed, and flexibility. This type of fitness is affected by physical maturity, as well as strength training and other types of training. Your athletes will likely exhibit a relatively wide range of muscular fitness. Those who have greater muscular fitness will be able to wrestle with great success. They will also sustain fewer muscular injuries, and any injuries that do occur will tend to be more minor in nature. In case of injury, the recovery rate is accelerated in those with higher levels of muscular fitness.

Two other components of fitness and injury prevention are the warmup and the cool-down. Although young bodies are generally very limber, they can get tight from inactivity. The warm-up should address each muscle group and get the heart rate elevated in preparation for strenuous activity. Have athletes warm up for 5 minutes by playing easy games and stretching.

As practice winds down, slow athletes' heart rates with an easy jog or walk. Then have athletes stretch for 5 minutes to help avoid stiff muscles and make them less tight before the next practice or match.

Equipment and Facilities Inspection

Another way to prevent injuries is to regularly examine the facilities in which your athletes practice and compete. Remove hazards, report conditions you cannot remedy, and request maintenance as necessary. If unsafe conditions exist, either make adaptations to avoid risk to your athletes' safety or stop the practice or match until safe conditions have been restored.

Athlete Matchups and Inherent Risks

We recommend that you group teams in 2-year age ranges if possible. You'll encounter fewer mismatches in physical maturation with narrow age ranges. Even so, two 12-year-old boys might differ by 90 pounds in weight, a foot in height, and 3 or 4 years in emotional and intellectual maturity. This presents dangers for those who are less mature. Whenever possible, match athletes against opponents of similar size and physical maturity. Such an approach gives smaller, less mature youngsters a better chance to succeed and avoid injury while providing more mature athletes with a greater challenge. Closely supervise matches so that more mature athletes do not put less mature athletes at undue risk.

Proper matching helps protect you from certain liability concerns. But you must also warn athletes of the inherent risks involved in wrestling, because "failure to warn" is one of the most successful arguments in lawsuits against coaches. So, thoroughly explain the inherent risks of wrestling, and make sure each athlete knows, understands, and appreciates those risks.

The preseason parent-orientation meeting is a good opportunity to explain the risks of the sport to both parents and athletes. It is also a good occasion on which to have both the athletes and their parents sign waivers releasing you from liability should an injury occur. Such waivers do not relieve you of responsibility for your athletes' well-being, but they are recommended by lawyers.

Proper Supervision and Record Keeping

To ensure athletes' safety, you will need to provide both general supervision and specific supervision. General supervision requires your being in the area of activity so that you can see and hear what is happening. You should be

- immediately accessible to the activity and able to oversee the entire activity,
- alert to conditions that may be dangerous to athletes and ready to take action to protect them, and
- able to react immediately and appropriately to emergencies.

Specific supervision is direct supervision of an activity at practice. For example, you should provide specific supervision when you teach new skills and continue it until your athletes understand the requirements of the activity, the risks involved, and their own ability to perform in light of these risks. You need to also provide specific supervision when you notice either athletes breaking rules or a change in the condition of your athletes.

As a general rule, the more dangerous the activity, the more specific the supervision required. This suggests that more specific supervision is required with younger and less experienced athletes.

As part of your supervision duty, you are expected to foresee potentially dangerous situations and be positioned to help prevent them from occurring. This requires that you know wrestling well, especially the rules that are intended to provide for safety. Prohibit dangerous horseplay, and hold practices and matches only under safe weather conditions (e.g., cancel practice if severe winter weather is forecast). These specific supervisory activities, applied consistently, will make the wrestling environment safer for your athletes and will help protect you from liability if a mishap does occur.

Environmental Conditions

Most problems due to environmental factors are related to excessive heat, although you should also consider other environmental factors such as pollution. A little thought about the potential problems and a little effort to ensure adequate protection for your athletes will prevent most serious emergencies that are related to environmental conditions.

Heat

On hot, humid days the body has difficulty cooling itself. Because the air is already saturated with water vapor (humidity), sweat doesn't evaporate as easily. Therefore, body sweat is a less effective cooling agent, and the body retains extra heat. Hot, humid environments make athletes prone to heat exhaustion and heatstroke (see more on these under "Serious Injuries" later in this chapter). If you think it's hot or humid, it's worse on the kids—not only because they're more active, but also because youngsters under the age of 12 have a more difficult time than adults regulating their body temperature. To provide for athletes' safety in hot or humid conditions, take the following preventive measures.

⊙ **Monitor weather conditions and adjust practices accordingly.** Figure 3.1 (page 22) shows the specific air temperatures and humidity percentages that can be hazardous.

⊙ **Acclimatize athletes to exercising in high heat and humidity.** Athletes can make adjustments to high heat and humidity over 7 to 10 days. During this time, hold practices at low to moderate activity levels and give the athletes water breaks every 20 minutes.

⊙ **Have athletes switch to light clothing.** Athletes should wear shorts and white t-shirts.

⊙ **Identify and monitor athletes who are prone to heat illness.** Athletes who are overweight, heavily muscled, or out of shape will be more prone to heat illness, as are athletes who work excessively hard or who have suffered heat illness before. Closely monitor these athletes and give them water breaks every 15 to 20 minutes.

⊙ **Make sure athletes replace water lost through sweat.** Encourage your athletes to drink 1 liter of water each day outside of practice and contest times, to drink 8 ounces of water every 20 minutes during practice or competition, and to drink 4 to 8 ounces of water 20 minutes before practice or competition.

⊙ **Encourage athletes to replenish electrolytes lost through sweat.** Sodium and potassium are lost through sweat. The best way to replace these nutrients is by eating a normal diet that contains fresh fruits and vegetables.

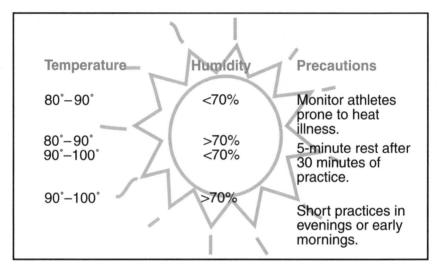

Temperature	Humidity	Precautions
80°–90°	<70%	Monitor athletes prone to heat illness.
80°–90°	>70%	
90°–100°	<70%	5-minute rest after 30 minutes of practice.
90°–100°	>70%	Short practices in evenings or early mornings.

Figure 3.1   Be sure to monitor weather conditions.

Water, Water Everywhere

Encourage athletes to drink plenty of water before, during, and after practice. Because water makes up 45–65% of a youngster's body weight and water weighs about a pound per pint, the loss of even a little bit of water can have severe consequences for the body's systems. It doesn't have to be hot and humid for athletes to become dehydrated. Nor do athletes have to feel thirsty; in fact, by the time they are aware of their thirst, they are long overdue for a drink.

Air Pollution

Poor air quality and smog can present real dangers to your athletes, even indoors. Both short- and long-term lung damage are possible from participating in unsafe air. While it's true that participating in clean air is not possible in many areas, restricting activity is recommended when the air-quality ratings are worse than moderate or when there is a smog alert. Your local health department or air-quality control board can inform you of the air-quality ratings for your area and when restricting activities is recommended.

Responding to Athletes' Injuries

No matter how good and thorough your prevention program is, injuries may occur. When injury does strike, chances are you will be the one in charge. The severity and nature of the injury will determine how actively involved you'll be in treating the injury. But regardless of how seriously an athlete is hurt, it is your responsibility to know what steps to take. So let's look at how you should prepare to provide basic emergency care to your injured athletes and take the appropriate action when an injury does occur.

Being Prepared

Being prepared to provide basic emergency care involves three steps: being trained in cardiopulmonary resuscitation (CPR) and first aid, having an appropriately stocked first-aid kit on hand at practices and matches, and having an emergency plan.

CPR and First-Aid Training

We recommend that all coaches receive CPR and first-aid training from a nationally recognized organization (the National Safety Council, the American Heart Association, the American Red Cross, or the American Sport Education Program). You should be certified based on a practical test and a written test of knowledge. CPR training should include pediatric and adult basic life support and obstructed airway procedures.

First-Aid Kit

A well-stocked first-aid kit should include the following:

- List of emergency phone numbers
- Change for a pay phone

- Face shield (for rescue breathing and CPR)
- Bandage scissors
- Plastic bags for crushed ice
- 3-inch and 4-inch elastic wraps
- Triangular bandages
- Sterile gauze pads—3-inch and 4-inch squares
- Saline solution for eyes
- Contact lens case
- Mirror
- Penlight
- Tongue depressors
- Cotton swabs
- Butterfly strips
- Bandage strips—assorted sizes
- Alcohol or peroxide
- Antibacterial soap
- First-aid cream or antibacterial ointment
- Petroleum jelly
- Tape adherent and tape remover
- 1 1/2-inch white athletic tape
- Prewrap
- Sterile gauze rolls
- Safety pins
- 1/8-inch, 1/4-inch, and 1/2-inch foam rubber
- Disposable surgical gloves
- Thermometer
- Special nose plugs for bloody noses
- Anti-fungal ointment or spray

Emergency Plan

An emergency plan is the final step in preparing to take appropriate action for severe or serious injuries. The plan calls for three steps:

1. **Evaluate the injured athlete.** Your CPR and first-aid training will guide you here.

2. **Call the appropriate medical personnel.** If possible, delegate the responsibility of seeking medical help to another calm and responsible adult who is on hand for all practices and matches. Write out a list of emergency phone numbers and keep it with you at practices and matches. Include the following phone numbers:

- Rescue unit
- Hospital
- Physician
- Police
- Fire department

Take each athlete's emergency information to every practice and match. (See appendix B.) This information includes the person to contact in case of an emergency, what types of medications the athlete is using, what types of drugs he or she is allergic to, and so on.

Give an emergency response card (see appendix C) to the contact person calling for emergency assistance. This provides the information the contact person needs to convey and will help keep the person calm, knowing that everything he or she needs to communicate is on the card. Also, complete an injury-report form (see appendix A) and keep it on file for any injury that occurs.

3. **Provide first aid.** If medical personnel are not on hand at the time of the injury, you should provide first-aid care to the extent of your qualifications. Again, while your CPR and first-aid training will guide you here, the following are important guidelines:

- Do not move the injured athlete if the injury is to the head, neck, or back; if a large joint (ankle, knee, elbow, shoulder) is dislocated; or if the pelvis, a rib, or an arm or leg is fractured.
- Calm the injured athlete and keep others away from him or her as much as possible.
- Evaluate whether the athlete's breathing is stopped or irregular, and if necessary, clear the airway with your fingers.
- Administer artificial respiration if the athlete's breathing has stopped. Administer CPR if the athlete's circulation has stopped.
- Remain with the athlete until medical personnel arrive.

Emergency Steps

Your emergency plan should follow this sequence:

1. Check the athlete's level of consciousness.

2. Send a contact person to call the appropriate medical personnel and to call the athlete's parents.

3. Send someone to wait for the rescue team and direct them to the injured athlete.

4. Assess the injury.

5. Administer first aid.

6. Assist emergency medical personnel in preparing the athlete for transportation to a medical facility.

7. Appoint someone to go with the athlete if his or her own parents are not available. This person should be responsible, calm, and familiar with the athlete. Assistant coaches or other athlete's parents are best for this job.

8. Complete an injury-report form while the incident is fresh in your mind. (See appendix A.)

Taking Appropriate Action

Proper CPR and first-aid training, a well-stocked first-aid kit, and an emergency plan help prepare you to take appropriate action when an injury occurs. We spoke in the previous section about the importance of providing first aid to the extent of your qualifications. Don't "play doctor" with injuries; sort out minor injuries that you can treat from those for which you need to call for medical assistance.

Next we'll look at taking the appropriate action for minor injuries and more serious injuries.

Minor Injuries

Although no injury seems minor to the person experiencing it, most injuries are neither life-threatening nor severe enough to restrict participation. When such injuries occur, you can take an active role in their initial treatment.

Scrapes and Cuts. When one of your athletes has an open wound, the first thing you should do is put on a pair of disposable surgical gloves or some other effective blood barrier. Then follow these four steps:

1. *Stop the bleeding* by applying direct pressure with a clean dressing to the wound and elevating it. The athlete may be able to apply this pressure while you put on your gloves. Do not remove the dressing if it becomes soaked with blood. Instead, place an additional dressing on top of the one already in place. If bleeding continues, elevate the injured area above the heart and maintain pressure.

2. *Cleanse the wound* thoroughly once the bleeding is controlled. A good rinsing with a forceful stream of water, and perhaps light scrubbing with soap, will help prevent infection.

3. *Protect the wound* with sterile gauze or a bandage strip. If the athlete continues to participate, apply protective padding over the injured area.

4. *Remove and dispose of gloves* carefully to prevent you or anyone else from coming into contact with blood.

For bloody noses not associated with serious facial injury, have the athlete sit and lean slightly forward. Then pinch the athlete's nostrils shut. If the bleeding continues after several minutes, or if the athlete has a history of nosebleeds, seek medical assistance.

Treating Bloody Injuries

You shouldn't let a fear of acquired immunodeficiency syndrome (AIDS) stop you from helping an athlete. You are only at risk if you allow contaminated blood to come in contact with an open wound, so the surgical disposable gloves that you wear will protect you from AIDS should one of your athletes carry this disease. Check with your director or your organization for more information about protecting yourself and your participants from AIDS.

Strains and Sprains. The physical demands of wrestling practices and matches often result in injury to the muscles or tendons (strains) or to the ligaments (sprains). When your athletes suffer minor strains or sprains, immediately apply the PRICE method of injury care:

P – Protect the athlete and injured body part from further danger or trauma.

R – Rest the area to avoid further damage and foster healing.

I – Ice the area to reduce swelling and pain.

C – Compress the area by securing an ice bag in place with an elastic wrap.

E – Elevate the injury above heart level to keep the blood from pooling in the area.

Bumps and Bruises. Inevitably, wrestlers make contact with each other and with the mat. If the force applied to a body part at impact is great enough, a bump or bruise will result. Many athletes continue playing with such sore spots, but if the bump or bruise is large and painful, you should act appropriately. Use the PRICE method for injury care and monitor the injury. If swelling, discoloration, and pain have lessened, the athlete may resume participation with protective padding; if not, the athlete should be examined by a physician.

Serious Injuries

Head, neck, and back injuries; fractures; and injuries that cause an athlete to lose consciousness are among a class of injuries that you cannot and should not try to treat yourself. In these cases you should follow the emergency plan outlined earlier. We do want to examine more closely your role, however, in preventing and handling two heat illnesses: heat exhaustion and heatstroke.

Heat Exhaustion. Heat exhaustion is a shocklike condition caused by dehydration and electrolyte depletion. Symptoms include headache, nausea, dizziness, chills, fatigue, and extreme thirst. Profuse sweating is a key sign of heat exhaustion. Other signs include pale, cool, and clammy skin; rapid, weak pulse; loss of coordination; and dilated pupils. See figure 3.2 for signs and symptoms of heat exhaustion.

An athlete suffering from heat exhaustion should rest in a cool, shaded area; drink cool water; and have ice applied to the neck, back, or abdomen to help cool the body. You may have to administer CPR if necessary or send for emergency medical assistance if the athlete doesn't recover or the condition worsens. Under no conditions should the athlete return to activity that day or before regaining all the weight lost through sweat. If the athlete has to see a physician, he shouldn't return to the team until he has a written release from the physician.

Heatstroke. Heatstroke is a life-threatening condition in which the body stops sweating and body temperature rises dangerously high. It occurs when dehydration causes a malfunction in the body's temperature control center in the brain. Symptoms include the feeling of being on fire (extremely hot), nausea, confusion, irritability, and fatigue. Signs include hot, dry, and flushed or red skin (this is a key sign); lack of sweat; rapid pulse; rapid breathing; constricted pupils; vomiting; diarrhea; and possibly seizures, unconsciousness, or respiratory or cardiac arrest. See figure 3.2 for signs and symptoms of heatstroke.

Send for emergency medical assistance immediately and have the athlete rest in a cool area. Remove excess clothing and equipment from the athlete, and cool the athlete's body with cool, wet towels or by pouring cool water over him or her. Apply ice packs to the armpits, neck, back, and abdomen, and between the legs. If the athlete is conscious, have him drink cool water. If the athlete is unconscious, place him on his side to allow fluids and vomit to drain from the mouth.

An athlete who has suffered heatstroke should not be allowed to return to the team without a written release from a physician.

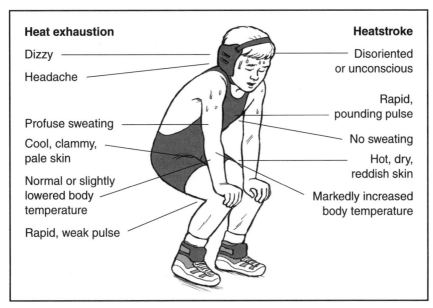

Figure 3.2 Signs of heat exhaustion and heatstroke.

Protecting Yourself

When one of your athletes is injured, naturally your first concern is his or her well-being. Your feelings for youngsters, after all, are what made you decide to coach. Unfortunately, there is something else that you must consider: Can you be held liable for the injury?

From a legal standpoint, a coach has the following nine duties to fulfill:

1. Provide a safe environment.
2. Properly plan the activity.
3. Provide adequate and proper equipment.

4. Match, or equate, athletes.

5. Warn of inherent risks in the sport.

6. Supervise the activity closely.

7. Evaluate athletes for injury or incapacitation.

8. Know emergency procedures and first aid.

9. Keep adequate records.

We've discussed all but number 3 in this chapter.

In order to protect yourself legally, keep records of your season plans, practice plans, and athletes' injuries. Season and practice plans come in handy when you need evidence that athletes have been taught certain skills, whereas accurate, detailed injury-report forms offer protection against unfounded lawsuits. Ask for these forms from your sponsoring organization (appendix A has a sample injury-report form), and hold on to these records for several years so that an "old wrestling injury" of a former athlete doesn't come back to haunt you.

In addition to fulfilling the nine legal duties outlined earlier, you should check your organization's insurance coverage and your insurance coverage to make sure these policies will protect you from liability.

chapter 4

The Games Approach to Coaching Wrestling

Do you remember how as a kid you were taught by adults to play a sport, either in an organized sport program or physical education class? They probably taught you the basic skills using a series of drills that, if the truth be known, you found very boring. As you began to learn the basic skills, they eventually taught you the tactics of the game, showing you when to use these skills in various game situations. Do you remember how impatient you became during what seemed to be endless instruction, and how much you just wanted to play? Well, forget this traditional approach to teaching sport.

Now can you recall learning a sport by playing with a group of your friends in the neighborhood? You didn't learn the basic skills first; no time for that. You began playing immediately. If you didn't know the basic things to do, your friends told you quickly during the game so that they could keep playing. We're going to ask you to use a very similar approach to teaching wrestling to young people called the games approach, an approach we think knocks the socks off the traditional approach.

On the surface, it would seem to make sense to introduce wrestling by first teaching the basic skills of the sport and then the tactics, but we've discovered that this approach has disadvantages. First, it teaches the skills of wrestling out of the context of the match. Kids may learn to shoot and sprawl, but they find it difficult to use these skills in a real match. This is because they do not yet understand the fundamental tactics of wrestling and do not appreciate how best to use their newfound skills.

Second, learning skills by doing drills outside of the context of wrestling is so-o-o-o boring. The single biggest turnoff about adults teaching kids sport is that we overorganize the instruction and deprive kids of their intrinsic desire to wrestle.

We're asking that you clear the traditional approach out of your mind and teach wrestling the games approach way. Once you fully understand this approach, you'll quickly see its superiority in teaching wrestling. Not only will kids learn to wrestle better, but also you and your athletes will have much more fun. As a bonus, you'll have far fewer discipline problems.

The games approach begins with wrestling . These will be modified versions of wrestling designed to suit the age and ability of the athletes. As the kids play in these "mini" games, they begin to understand the nature of wrestling and to appreciate simple concepts of positioning and tactics. When your athletes understand what they must do in the games, they are then eager to develop the skills to wrestle. Now that athletes are motivated to learn the skills, you can demonstrate wrestling skills, practice using gamelike drills, and provide individual instruction by identifying athletes' errors and helping to correct them.

In the traditional approach to teaching sports, athletes do this:

Learn the skill → Learn the tactics → Play the game

Figure 4.1 demonstrates what athletes do in the games approach to learning sports.

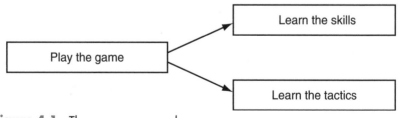

Figure 4.1 The games approach.

In the past we have placed too much emphasis on the learning of skills and not enough on learning how to play skillfully—that is, how to use those skills in competition. The games approach, in contrast, emphasizes learning what to do first, then how to do it. Moreover—and this is a really important point—the games approach lets kids discover what to do not by your telling them, but by their experiencing it. What you do as an effective coach is help them discover what they've experienced.

In contrast to the "skill-drill-kill-the-enthusiasm" approach, the games approach is a guided discovery method of teaching. It empowers your kids to solve the problems that arise in the match, and that's a big part of the fun of learning wrestling.

Let's look more closely at the games approach to see the four-step process for teaching wrestling:

1. Play a modified wrestling game.

2. Help the athletes discover what they need to do to play the game successfully.

3. Teach wrestling skills.

4. Practice the skills in another game.

Step 1: Play a Modified Wrestling Game

OK, it's the first day of practice; some of the kids are eager to get started, while others are obviously apprehensive. Some have rarely seen real amateur wrestling, and most don't know the rules. What do you do?

If you use the traditional approach, you start with a little warm-up activity, then line the athletes up for a simple penetration step drill and go from there. With the games approach, you begin by playing a modified game that is developmentally appropriate for the level of the athletes and also designed to focus on learning a specific part of wrestling.

Modified wrestling emphasizes a limited number of situations. This is one way you "guide" your athletes to discover certain tactics in wrestling. For instance, you have your athletes participate in a sumo drill, in which two participants try to move each other out of an 8-foot circle. Playing this way teaches the athletes about balance and control while attacking their opponent. Wrestling this way forces athletes to think about what they have to do to set up an effective attack.

Step 2: Help the Athletes Discover What They Need to Do

As your athletes are playing the game, look for the right spot to "freeze" the action, step in, and hold a brief question-and-answer session to discuss problems they were having in carrying out the goals of the game. You don't need to pop in on the first miscue, but if they repeat the same types of mental or physical mistakes a few times in a row, step in and ask them questions that relate to the aim of the game and the necessary skills required. The best time to interrupt the game is when you notice that they are having trouble carrying out the main goal, or aim, of the game. By stopping the game, freezing action, and asking questions, you'll help them understand

- the aim of the game,
- what they must do to achieve that aim, and
- what skills they must use to achieve that aim.

For example, if your athletes are playing a game in which the focus is on keeping the opponent broken down flat to his stomach, but they are having trouble maintaining that good breakdown position, interrupt the action and ask the following questions:

Coach: What are you supposed to do in this game?

Athletes: Keep the bottom wrestler on his stomach.

Coach: How do you do that?

Athletes: By chopping his arms or picking his ankles, and by maintaining pressure on top.

Coach: Yes, and what else?

Athletes: You have to keep weight on him, too.

Coach: OK. Chop his arms, pick his ankles, and keep weight on him. Now why don't we work on the breakdown position?

Through the modified game and skillful questioning on your part, your athletes realize that maintaining a breakdown is essential to their success in going for a fall. Just as important, rather than telling them that breakdown skills are critical, you led them to that discovery through a well-designed modified game and through questions. This questioning that leads to athletes' discovery is a crucial part of the games approach. Essentially you'll be asking your athletes—usually literally— "What do you need to do to succeed in this situation?"

Asking the right questions is a very important part of your coaching. At first, asking questions will be difficult because your athletes have little or no experience with wrestling. In addition, if you've learned sport through the traditional approach, you'll be tempted to tell your athletes how to wrestle and not waste time asking them questions. Resist this powerful temptation to tell them what to do, and especially don't do so before they begin to play the game.

If your athletes have trouble understanding what to do, phrase your questions to let them choose between two options. For example, if you ask them, "What's the better position for your head when you shoot a double-leg?" and get answers such as, "Have your head to the inside of the body," then ask, "Is it better to have your head on his hip or between his legs?"

Immediately following the question-and-answer session you will begin a skill practice, which is step 3 of the four-step process.

Sometimes athletes simply need to have more time playing the game, or you may need to modify the game further so that it is even easier for them to discover what they are to do. It'll take more patience on your part, but it's a powerful way to learn.

Step 3: Teach Wrestling Skills

Only when your athletes recognize the skills they need to be successful do you want to teach the specific skills through focused drills. This is when you use a more traditional approach to teaching sport skills, the IDEA approach, which we will describe in chapter 5.

Step 4: Practice the Skills in Another Game

Once the athletes have practiced the skill, put them in another game situation to let them practice the skill in the context of a game.

That's the games approach. Your athletes will get to wrestle more in practice, and once they learn how the skills fit into their performance and enjoyment of wrestling, they'll be more motivated to work on those skills, which will help them to be successful.

Teaching and Shaping Skills

Coaching wrestling is about teaching tactics, skills, fitness, values, and other useful things. It's also about coaching athletes before, during, and after matches. Teaching and coaching are closely related, but there are important differences. In this chapter we'll focus on principles of teaching, especially on teaching wrestling skills. But many of the principles we'll discuss apply to teaching tactics, fitness concepts, and values—all elements of our curriculum. (Most of the other important teaching principles deal with communication, covered in chapter 2.) Then in chapter 6 we'll discuss the principles of coaching, which refer to your leadership activities during matches.

Teaching Wrestling Skills

Many people believe that the only qualification needed to teach a skill is to have performed it. It's helpful to have performed it, but there is much more than that to teaching successfully. Moreover, even if you haven't performed the skill before, you can still learn to teach successfully with the useful acronym IDEA:

I – Introduce the skill.

D – Demonstrate the skill.

E – Explain the skill.

A – Attend to athletes practicing the skill.

These are the basic steps of good teaching. Now we'll explain each step in greater detail.

Introduce the Skill

Athletes, especially young and inexperienced ones, need to know what skill they are learning and why they are learning it. You should therefore take these three steps every time you introduce a skill to your athletes:

1. Get your athletes' attention.
2. Name the skill.
3. Explain the importance of the skill.

Get Your Athletes' Attention

Because youngsters are easily distracted, use some method to get their attention. Some coaches use interesting news items or stories. Others use jokes. Still others simply project enthusiasm to get their athletes to listen. Whatever method you use, speak slightly above the normal volume and look your athletes in the eyes when you speak.

Also, position athletes so that they can see and hear you. Arrange the athletes in two or three evenly spaced rows, facing you. (Make sure they aren't looking at some distracting activity behind you.) Then ask if all of them can see you before you begin.

Name the Skill

Although you might mention multiple names for the skill, decide which one you'll use and stick with it. This will help avoid confusion and enhance communication among your athletes.

Explain the Importance of the Skill

Although the importance of a skill may be apparent to you, your athletes may be less able to see how the skill will help them become better wrestlers. Offer them a reason for learning the skill and describe how the skill relates to more advanced skills.

> The most difficult aspect of coaching is this: Coaches must learn to let athletes learn. Sport skills should be taught so that they have meaning to the child, not just meaning to the coach.
>
> —Rainer Martens, founder of the American Sport Education Program

Demonstrate the Skill

The demonstration step is the most important part of teaching sport skills to athletes who may never have done anything closely resembling the skill. They need a picture, not just words. They need to see how the skill is performed.

If you are unable to perform the skill correctly, have an assistant coach, one of your athletes, or someone else more skilled perform the demonstration. These tips will help make your demonstrations more effective:

- Use correct form.
- Demonstrate the skill several times.
- Slow down the action, if possible, during one or two performances so that athletes can see every movement involved in the skill.
- Perform the skill at different angles so that your athletes can get a full perspective of it.
- Demonstrate the skill with both the right and the left arms or legs.

Explain the Skill

Athletes learn more effectively when they're given a brief explanation of the skill along with the demonstration. Use simple terms and, if possible, relate the skill to previously learned skills. Ask your athletes whether they understand your description. A good technique is to ask the team to repeat your explanation. Ask questions such as, "What are you going to do first?" and "Then what?" Watch for when athletes look confused or uncertain and repeat your explanation and demonstration at those points. If possible, use different words so that your athletes get a chance to try to understand the skill from different perspectives.

Complex skills often are better understood when they are explained in more manageable parts. For instance, if you want to teach your athletes how to shoot a hi-c or high-crotch takedown, you might follow these steps:

1. Show them a correct performance of the entire skill, and explain its function in wrestling.
2. Break down the skill and point out its component parts.
3. Have athletes perform each of the component skills you have already taught them, such as the setup, the level change, the proper hand position on the leg, and the finish or lift.
4. After athletes have demonstrated their ability to perform the separate parts of the skill in sequence, reexplain the entire skill.
5. Have athletes practice the skill in matchlike conditions.

One caution: Because young athletes have short attention spans, a long demonstration or explanation of the skill will bore them. Spend no more than a few minutes altogether on the introduction, demonstration, and explanation phases. Then get the athletes active in a game that calls on them to perform the skill. The total IDEA should be completed in 10 minutes or less, followed by games in which athletes practice the skill.

Attend to Athletes Practicing the Skill

If the skill you selected was within your athletes' capabilities and you have done an effective job of introducing, demonstrating, and explaining it, your athletes should be ready to attempt the skill. Some athletes may need to be guided physically through the movements during their first few attempts. Walking unsure athletes through the skill in this way will help them gain confidence to perform the skill on their own.

Your teaching duties don't end when all your athletes have demonstrated that they understand how to perform the skill. In fact, a significant part of your teaching will involve observing closely the hit-and-miss trial performances of your athletes. In the next section we'll guide you in shaping athletes' skills, and then we'll help you learn how to detect and correct errors using positive feedback. Keep in mind that your feedback will have a great influence on your athletes' motivation to practice and improve their performances.

Remember, too, that athletes need individual instruction. So set aside a time before, during, or after practice to give individual help.

Helping Athletes Improve Skills

After you have successfully taught your athletes the fundamentals of a skill, your focus will be on helping them improve that skill. Athletes will learn skills and improve on them at different rates, so don't get too frustrated. Instead, help them improve by shaping their skills and detecting and correcting errors.

Shaping Athletes' Skills

One of your principal teaching duties is to reward positive behavior—in terms of successful skill execution—when you see it. An athlete takes a good shot in practice, and you immediately say, "Good shot! Way to set up your shot and drive through the finish—nice job of staying off your knees." This, plus a smile and a thumbs-up gesture, go a long way toward reinforcing that technique in that athlete.

However, sometimes you may have a long dry spell before you have any correct technique to reinforce. It's difficult to reward athletes when they aren't executing skills correctly. How can you shape their skills if this is the case?

Shaping skills takes practice on your athletes' part and patience on your part. Expect your athletes to make errors. Telling the athlete who made the great shot that he did a good job doesn't ensure that he'll make that takedown next time. Seeing inconsistency in your athletes' techniques can be frustrating. It's even more challenging to stay positive when your athletes repeatedly perform a skill incorrectly or lack enthusiasm for learning. It can certainly be frustrating to see athletes who seemingly don't heed your advice and continue to make the same mistakes. When the athletes don't seem to care, you may wonder why you should.

Please know that it is normal to get frustrated at times when teaching skills. Nevertheless, part of successful coaching is controlling this frustration. Instead of getting upset, use these six guidelines for shaping skills:

1. Think small initially. Reward the first signs of behavior that approximate what you want. Then reward closer and closer approximations of the desired behavior. In short, use your reward power to shape the behavior you seek.

2. Break skills into small steps. For instance, in learning to defend a double-leg shot, one of your athletes does well with her sprawl, but her cross-face is inconsistent. Reinforce the correct technique of her sprawl, and teach her how to make more consistent cross-faces. When she masters that, focus on getting her to go behind for the takedown quickly.

3. Develop one component of a skill at a time. Don't try to shape two components of a skill at once. For example, while hitting a switch, athletes must first clear their arm, then move their hips away from their opponent in a side hip-heist. Athletes should focus first on one aspect (clearing the arm), then on the other (moving the hips away from the opponent in a side hip-heist). Athletes who have problems mastering a skill often are trying to improve two or more components at once. Help these athletes to isolate a single component.

4. As athletes become more proficient at a skill, reinforce them only occasionally and only for the best examples of the skill behavior. By focusing only on the best examples, you will help them continue to improve once they've mastered the basics.

5. When athletes are trying to master a new skill, temporarily relax your standards for how you reward them. As they focus on the new skill or attempt to integrate it with other skills, don't be surprised if the old well-learned skills temporarily degenerate. This is normal.

6. If, however, a well-learned skill degenerates for long, you may need to restore it by going back to the basics.

Coaches often have more skilled athletes provide feedback to teammates as they practice skills. This can be effective, but proceed with caution: You must tell the skilled athletes exactly what to look for when their teammates are performing the skills. You must also teach them the corrections for the common errors of that skill.

We've looked at how to guide your athletes as they learn skills. Now let's look at another critical teaching principle that you should employ as you're shaping skills: detecting and correcting errors.

Detecting and Correcting Errors

Good coaches recognize that athletes make two types of errors: learning errors and performance errors. Learning errors are ones that occur because athletes don't know how to perform a skill; that is, they have not yet developed the correct motor program in the brain to perform a particular skill. Performance errors are made not because athletes don't know how to do the skill, but because they make a mistake in executing what they do know. There is no easy way to know whether an athlete is making learning or performance errors. Part of the art of coaching is being able to sort out which type of error is occurring.

The process of helping your athletes correct errors begins with your observing and evaluating their performances to determine if the mistakes are learning or performance errors. For performance errors, you need to look for the reasons that your athletes are not performing as well as they know how. If the mistakes are learning errors, then you need to help them learn the skill, which is the focus of this section.

There is no substitute for knowing skills well in correcting learning errors. The better you understand a skill—not only how it is done correctly but also what causes learning errors—the more helpful you will be in correcting mistakes.

One of the most common coaching mistakes is providing inaccurate feedback and advice on how to correct errors. Don't rush into error correction; wrong feedback or poor advice will hurt the learning process more than no feedback or advice. If you are uncertain about the cause of the problem or how to correct it, continue to observe and analyze until you are more sure. As a rule, you should see the error repeated several times before attempting to correct it.

Correct One Error at a Time

Suppose Jack, one of your athletes, is having trouble with his front headlock. He's doing most things well, but you notice that he's not scoring as quickly or as easily as he should be from this position. He gets to the position quickly, and his shoulder is pressuring the center of his opponent's back, and he also has control of his opponent's chin. But often when Jack gets to the front headlock, he loses his footing and drops to his knee, sometimes just to adjust into position but long enough to keep him from getting control of his opponent's near arm. This leads to Jack being unable to spin quickly behind for the takedown, as his opponent is adjusting to the position. What do you do?

Because athletes learn more effectively when they attempt to correct one error at a time, decide which error to correct first. Determine whether one error is causing the other; if so, have the athlete correct that error first because it may eliminate the other error. In Jack's case, dropping to his knees may cause him to miss controlling the near arm, so you should correct his dropping to his knees first. When neither error is necessarily causing the other, correct the error that will bring the greatest improvement when remedied. Correcting one error often motivates athletes to correct other errors.

Use Positive Feedback to Correct Errors

The positive approach to correcting errors includes emphasizing what to do instead of what not to do. Use compliments, praise, rewards, and encouragement to correct errors. Acknowledge correct performance as well as efforts to improve. By using the positive approach, you can help your athletes feel good about themselves and promote a strong desire to achieve.

When you're working with one athlete at a time, the positive approach to correcting errors includes four steps:

1. Praise effort and correct performance.
2. Give simple and precise feedback to correct errors.
3. Make sure the athlete understands your feedback.
4. Provide an environment that motivates the athlete to improve.

Let's take a brief look at each step.

Step 1: Praise Effort and Correct Performance. Praise your athlete for trying to perform a skill correctly and for performing any parts of it correctly. Praise the athlete immediately after he or she performs the skill, if possible. Keep the praise simple: "Good try," "Way to hustle," "Good stance," "Good position," or "That's the way to drive through." You can also use nonverbal feedback such as smiling, clapping your hands, or any facial or body expression that shows approval.

Make sure you're sincere with your praise. Don't indicate that an athlete's effort was good when it wasn't. Usually an athlete knows when he has made a sincere effort to perform the skill correctly and perceives undeserved praise for what it is—untruthful feedback to make him feel good. Likewise, don't indicate that an athlete's performance was correct when it wasn't.

Step 2: Give Simple and Precise Feedback. Don't burden an athlete with a long or detailed explanation of how to correct an error. Give just enough feedback so that the athlete can correct one error at a time. Before giving feedback, recognize that some athletes will readily accept it immediately after the error; others will respond better if you slightly delay the correction. Try to determine which type of athlete you're dealing with.

For errors that are complicated to explain and difficult to correct, try the following:

1. Explain and demonstrate what the athlete should have done. Do not demonstrate what the athlete did wrong.
2. Explain the cause or causes of the error, if it isn't obvious.
3. Explain why you are recommending the correction you have selected, if it's not obvious.

Step 3: Make Sure the Athlete Understands Your Feedback. If the athlete doesn't understand your feedback, he won't be able to correct the error. Ask him to repeat the feedback and to explain and demonstrate how it will be used. If the athlete can't do this, be patient and present your feedback again. Then have the athlete repeat the feedback after you're finished.

Step 4: Provide an Environment That Motivates the Athlete to Improve. Your athletes won't always be able to correct their errors immediately even if they do understand your feedback. Encourage them to "hang tough" and stick with it when corrections are difficult or they seem discouraged. For more difficult corrections, remind them that it will take time, and the improvement will happen only if they work at it. Look to encourage athletes with low self-confidence. Saying something like, "You were defending against the attacks much better today; with practice you'll be able to block those shots and set up your own attacks." Such feedback can motivate an athlete to continue to refine his skills.

Some athletes need to be more motivated to improve. Others may be very self-motivated and need little help from you in this area at all; with them you can practically ignore step 4 when correcting an error. While motivation comes from within, look to provide an environment of positive instruction and encouragement to help your athletes improve.

Developing Practice Plans

You will need to create practice plans for each season. Each practice plan should contain the following sections:

- Purpose
- Equipment
- Plan

Purpose sections focus on what you want to teach your athletes during each practice; they outline your main theme for each practice. The purpose should be drawn from your season plan (see chapter 10). Equipment sections note what you'll need to have on hand for that practice. Plan sections outline what you will do during each practice session. Each consists of these elements:

- Game
- Skill practice
- Cool-down and Review

Begin each session with about 5 minutes of warm-up activities. Then have your athletes play a modified wrestling game. (Look in chapter 9 for suggested games and chapter 10 for their use in season plans.) Look for your cue to interrupt that game—your cue being when athletes are having problems with carrying out the basic goal or aim of the game. At this point "freeze" the action, keeping the athletes where they are, and ask brief questions about the tactical problems the athletes encountered and what skills they need to solve those problems. (Review chapter 4 for more on interrupting a game and holding a question-and-answer session.)

Next, teach the skill the athletes need to acquire to successfully execute the tactic. During skill practice you'll use the IDEA approach:

I – Introduce the skill.

D – Demonstrate the skill.

E – Explain the skill.

A – Attend to athletes practicing the skill.

Your introduction, demonstration, and explanation of a skill should take no more than 2 to 3 minutes; then you'll attend to athletes and provide teaching cues or further demonstration as necessary as they practice the skill.

After the skill practices, you will usually have the athletes play another game or two to let them use the skills they have just learned and to understand them in the context of a match. During game and skill practices, emphasize the importance of every athlete watching, coaching, and encouraging those participating in the game. Each athlete should be trying his absolute best to complete the activity with success and good technique.

The plan section continues with a cool-down and stretch. Following this you'll wrap up the practice with a few summary comments and remind them of the next practice or match day.

Chapter 9 includes suggestions to help you modify the games. These suggestions will help you keep practices fun and provide activities for athletes with varying skill levels.

Although practicing using the games approach should reduce the need for discipline, there will be times when you'll have to deal with athletes who are misbehaving in practice. In the next section we'll help you handle these situations.

Dealing With Misbehavior

Athletes will misbehave at times; it's only natural. Two ways you can respond to misbehavior are through extinction or discipline.

Extinction

Ignoring a misbehavior—neither rewarding nor disciplining it—is called extinction. This can be effective under certain circumstances. In some situations, disciplining young people's misbehavior only encourages them to act up further because of the recognition they get. Ignoring misbehavior teaches youngsters that it is not worth your attention.

Sometimes, though, you cannot wait for a behavior to fizzle out. When athletes cause danger to themselves or others or disrupt the activities of others, you need to take immediate action. Tell the offending athlete that the behavior must stop and that discipline will follow if it doesn't. If the athlete doesn't stop misbehaving after the warning, discipline.

Extinction also doesn't work well when a misbehavior is self-rewarding. For example, you may be able to keep from grimacing if a youngster kicks you in the shin, but he or she still knows you were hurt. Therein lies the reward. In these circumstances, it is also necessary to discipline the athlete for the undesirable behavior.

Extinction works best in situations in which athletes are seeking recognition through mischievous behaviors, clowning, or grandstanding.

Usually, if you are patient, their failure to get your attention will cause the behavior to disappear.

However, be careful not to extinguish desirable behavior. When youngsters do something well, they expect to be positively reinforced. Not rewarding them will likely cause them to discontinue the desired behavior.

Discipline

Some educators say we should never discipline young people, but should only reinforce their positive behaviors. They argue that discipline does not work; rather, it creates hostility and sometimes develops avoidance behaviors that may be more unwholesome than the original problem behavior. It is true that discipline does not always work and that it can create problems when used ineffectively, but when used appropriately, discipline is effective in eliminating undesirable behaviors without creating other undesirable consequences. Because it is impossible to guide athletes through positive reinforcement and extinction alone, discipline has its place. It can be part of the positive approach when these guidelines are followed:

- Discipline in a corrective way to help athletes improve now and in the future. Don't discipline to retaliate and make yourself feel better.
- Impose discipline in an impersonal way when athletes break team rules or otherwise misbehave. Shouting at or scolding athletes indicates an attitude of revenge.
- Once a good rule has been agreed on, ensure that athletes who violate it experience the unpleasant consequences of their misbehavior. Don't wave discipline threateningly over their heads; just do it, but warn an athlete once first.
- Be consistent in administering discipline.
- Don't discipline using consequences that may cause you guilt. If you can't think of an appropriate consequence right away, tell the athlete you will talk with him after you think about it. You might consider involving the athlete in designing a consequence.
- Once the discipline is completed, don't make athletes feel they are "in the doghouse." Make them feel that they're valued members of the team again.
- Make sure that what you think is discipline isn't perceived by the athlete as a positive reinforcement—for instance, keeping an ath-

lete out of doing a certain drill or portion of the practice may be just what the athlete desired.

⊙ Never discipline athletes for making errors when they are playing.

⊙ Never use physical activity—running laps or doing push-ups—as discipline. Doing so only causes athletes to resent physical activity, something we want them to learn to enjoy throughout their lives.

⊙ Discipline sparingly. Constant discipline and criticism cause athletes to turn their interests elsewhere and to resent you as well.

chapter 6

Match-Day Coaching

Matches provide the opportunity for your athletes to show what they've learned in practice. Just as your athletes' focus shifts on match days from learning and practicing to competing, so your focus shifts from teaching skills to coaching athletes as they perform those skills in matches. Of course, the match is a teaching opportunity as well, but the focus is on performing what has been previously learned.

In the last chapter you learned how to teach your athletes wrestling tactics and skills; in this chapter we'll help you coach your athletes as they execute those tactics and skills in matches. We'll provide important coaching principles that will guide you throughout the match day—before, during, and after the match.

Before the Match

Just as you need a practice plan for what you're going to do each practice, you need a match plan for what to do on the day of a match. Many inexperienced coaches focus only on how they will coach during the match itself, but your preparations to coach should include details that begin well before the first blow of the whistle in the match. In fact, your preparations should begin during the practice before the match.

Preparations at Practice

During the practice a day or two before the next match, you should do two things (besides practicing tactics and skills) to prepare your athletes: Decide on any specific tactics that you want to employ; and discuss prematch particulars such as what to eat before the match, what to wear, and when to be at the tournament or match.

Deciding Team Tactics

Some coaches see themselves as great military strategists guiding their young warriors to victory on the battlefield. These coaches burn the midnight oil as they devise a complex plan of attack. Several things are wrong with this approach, but we'll point out two errors in terms of deciding tactics:

1. The decision on tactics should be made with input from athletes.
2. Tactics at this level don't need to be complex.

Perhaps you guessed right on the second point but were surprised by the first. Why should you include your athletes in deciding tactics? Isn't that the coach's role?

It's the coach's role to help youngsters grow through the sport experience. Giving your athletes input here helps them to learn wrestling. It gets them involved at a planning level that often is reserved solely for the coach. It gives them a feeling of ownership. They're not just carrying out the orders of the coach, they're also executing the plan of attack that was jointly decided. Youngsters who have a say in how they approach a task often respond with more enthusiasm and motivation.

Don't dampen that enthusiasm and motivation by concocting tactics that are too complex. Keep tactics simple, especially at the younger levels. Focus on simple setups or controlling specific contact positions such as underhooks.

As you become more familiar with your team's tendencies and abilities, help them focus on specific tactics that will help them wrestle better. For example, if your athletes have a tendency to stand up and relax or to come out of their stances at critical times during a match, you may want to emphasize the importance of staying in a tight position ready to shoot or react, especially on the edge of the mat.

If you're coaching 12- to 14-year-olds, you might institute certain moves that your team has practiced. These techniques should take advantage of your athletes' strengths. Again, give the athletes some input into what plays might be employed in a match.

Discussing Prematch Particulars

Athletes need to know what to do before a match: what they should eat on match day and when, what clothing they should wear to the match, what equipment they should bring, and what time they should arrive at the gym. Discuss these particulars with them at the practice before a match. Here are guidelines for discussing these issues.

Prematch Meal. Carbohydrates are easily digested and absorbed and are a ready source of fuel. Athletes should eat a high-carbohydrate meal ideally about 3 to 4 hours before a match to allow the stomach to empty completely. This won't be possible for matches held in the early morning; in this case, athletes should still eat food high in carbohydrates, such as an English muffin, toast, or cereal, but not so much that their stomachs are full. In addition, athletes' prematch meals shouldn't include foods that are spicy or high in fat content. Nutrition is discussed more fully in chapter 8.

Clothing and Equipment. Instruct athletes to wear singlets, head gear, wrestling shoes, and a team uniform or shirt.

Time to Arrive. Your athletes will need to adequately warm up before a match, so instruct them to arrive 20 minutes before a match to go through a team warm-up (see "The Warm-Up" later in this chapter).

Facilities, Equipment, and Support Personnel

Although the site coordinator and officials have responsibilities regarding facilities and equipment, it's wise for you to know what to look for to make sure the match is safe for the athletes. You should arrive at the gym 25 to 30 minutes before match time so that you can check the gym, check in with the site coordinator and officials, and greet your athletes as they arrive to warm up. The site coordinator and officials should be checking the facilities and preparing for the match. If officials aren't arriving before the match when they're supposed to, inform the site coordinator. A facilities checklist includes the following:

Gymnasium or Wrestling Room Facilities

✔ The stairs and corridors leading to the gym are well lit.

✔ The stairs and corridors are free of obstruction.

✔ The stairs and corridors are in good repair.

✔ Exits are well marked and illuminated.

✔ Exits are free of obstruction.

✔ Uprights and other projections are padded.

✔ Walls are free of projections.

✔ Windows are located high on the walls.

✔ Wall plugs and light switches are insulated and protected.

✔ Lights are shielded.

✔ Lighting is sufficient to illuminate the playing area well.

✔ The heating or cooling system for the gym is working properly and is monitored regularly.

✔ Ducts, radiators, pipes, and so on are shielded or designed to withstand high impact.

✔ Tamper-free thermostats are housed in impact-resistant covers.

✔ Gym equipment is inspected prior to and during each use.

✔ The gym is adequately supervised.

✔ Galleries and viewing areas have been designed to protect small children by blocking their access to the playing area.

✔ The gym (floor, roof, walls, light fixtures, etc.) is inspected on an annual basis for safety and structural deficiencies.

✔ Fire alarms are in good working order.

✔ Fire extinguishers are up to date, with a note of last inspection posted.

✔ Directions are posted for evacuating the gym in case of fire.

Communicating With Parents

The groundwork for your communication with parents will have been laid in the parent-orientation program, through which parents learn the best ways to support their kids'—and the team's—efforts in the gym. As parents gather in the gym before a match, let them know what the team has been focusing on during the past week and what your goals are for the match. For instance, if you've worked on arm drags in practice this week, encourage parents to watch for improvement and success in executing this tactic and to support the team members as they attempt all tactics and skills. Help parents to judge success not just based on the match outcome, but on how the kids are improving their performances.

Speak quietly to parents who yell at the kids for mistakes made during the match, make disparaging remarks about the officials or opponents, or shout instructions on what tactics to employ, asking them to refrain from making such remarks and to instead be supportive of the team in their comments and actions.

After a match, briefly and informally assess with parents, as the opportunity arises, how the team did based not on the outcome, but on meeting performance goals and wrestling to the best of their abilities. Help parents see the match as a process, not solely as a pass/fail or win/lose test. Encourage parents to reinforce that concept at home.

Unplanned Events

Part of being prepared to coach is to expect the unexpected. What do you do if athletes are late? What if you have an emergency and can't make the match or will be late? What if the match is postponed? Being prepared to handle out-of-the-ordinary circumstances will help you when such unplanned events happen.

If athletes are late, stress to them the importance of being on time for two reasons:

⊙ Part of being a member of a team means being committed and responsible to the other members. When athletes don't show up, or show up late, they break that commitment.

⊙ Athletes need to go through a warm-up to physically prepare for the match. Skipping the warm-up risks injury.

Consider making a team rule that athletes need to show up 20 minutes before a match and go through the complete team warm-up.

An emergency might cause you to be late or miss a match. In such cases, notify your assistant coach, if you have one, or the league coordinator. If notified in advance, a parent of an athlete or another volunteer might be able to step in for the match.

Sometimes a match will be postponed because of inclement weather or for other reasons (such as unsafe gym conditions). If the postponement takes place before match day, you'll need to call all the members of your team to let them know. If it happens while the teams are on the court preparing for the match, gather your team members and tell them the news and why the match is being postponed. Make sure all your athletes have rides home before you leave, and be the last to leave to be sure.

The Warm-Up

Athletes need to prepare both physically and mentally for a match once they arrive at the gym. Physical preparation involves warming up. We've suggested that athletes arrive 20 minutes before the match. Conduct the warm-up similar to practice warm-ups, with some brief games that focus on skill practice and stretching.

Athletes should prepare to do what they will do in the match: setup shots, sprawling, countering, hitting escapes and reversals, pinning combinations, and so on. This doesn't mean they spend extensive time on each skill; you can plan two or three brief practice games that encompass all these skills.

After playing a few brief games, your athletes should stretch. You don't need to deliver any big pep talk, but you can help your athletes mentally prepare as they stretch by reminding them of the following:

⊙ the tactics and skills they've been working on in recent practices, especially focusing their attention on what they've been doing well. Focus on their strengths.

⊙ the tactics you decided on in your previous practice.

⊙ performing the tactics and skills to the best of their individual abilities.

⊙ wrestling hard and smart, and having fun!

During the Match

The list you just read goes a long way toward defining your focus for coaching during the match. Throughout the match, you'll keep the competition in proper perspective and help your athletes do the same. You'll observe how your athletes execute tactics and skills. You'll make tactical decisions in a number of areas. You'll model appropriate behavior on the bench, showing respect for opponents and officials, and demand the same of your athletes. You'll watch out for your athletes' physical safety and psychological welfare, in terms of building their self-esteem and helping them manage stress and anxiety.

Proper Perspective

Winning matches is the short-term goal of your wrestling program; helping your athletes learn the skills and rules of wrestling, how to become fit, and how to be good sports in wrestling and in life are the long-term goals. Your young athletes are "winning" when they are becoming better human beings through their participation in wrestling. Keep that perspective in mind when you coach. You have the privilege of setting the tone for how your team approaches competition. Keep winning and all aspects of the competition in proper perspective, and your young charges will likely follow suit.

Tactical Decisions

While you aren't called to be a great military strategist, you are called to make tactical decisions in several areas throughout a match. You'll have to decide whether to make slight adjustments to your athletes' tactics, correct athletes' performance errors, or leave the correction for the next practice.

Adjusting Team Tactics

At the 8 to 9 and 10 to 11 age levels, you probably won't adjust athletes' tactics too significantly during a match; rather, you'll focus on the basic tactics in general and emphasize during breaks which tactics your athletes need to work on in particular. However, coaches of 12- to 14-year-olds might have cause to make tactical adjustments to improve their athletes' chances of performing well and winning. As the match progresses, assess your opponents' style of wrestling and make adjustments that are appropriate—that is, that your athletes are prepared for.

However, don't stress tactics too much during a match. Doing so can take the fun out of wrestling for the athletes. If you don't trust your memory, carry a pen and notepad to note which skills need attention in the next practice.

Correcting Athletes' Errors

In chapter 5 you learned about two types of errors: learning errors and performance errors. Learning errors are ones that occur because athletes don't know how to perform a skill. Athletes make performance errors not because they don't know how to do the skill, but because they make a mistake in executing what they do know.

Sometimes it's not easy to tell which type of error athletes are making. Knowing your athletes' capabilities helps you to know whether they know the skill and are simply making mistakes in executing it or whether they don't really know how to perform the skill. If they are making learning errors—that is, they don't know how to perform the skills—you'll need to make note of this and teach them at the next practice. Match time is not the time to teach skills.

If they are making performance errors, however, you can help athletes correct those errors between matches. Athletes who make performance errors often do so because they have a lapse in concentration or motivation—or they are simply demonstrating the human quality of sometimes doing things incorrectly. A word of encouragement to concentrate more may help. If you do correct a performance error during a match, do so in a quiet, controlled, and positive tone of voice during a break or when the athlete is on the bench with you.

For those making performance errors, you have to decide if it is just the occasional error anyone makes or an expected error for a youngster at that stage of development. If that is the case, then the athlete may appreciate your not commenting on the mistake. The athlete knows it was a mistake and knows how to correct it. On the other hand, perhaps an encouraging word and a "coaching cue" (such as "Remember to keep your elbows in and don't overextend your reach") may be just what the athlete needs. Knowing the athletes and what to say is very much a part of the art of coaching.

Coach's and Athletes' Behavior

Another aspect of coaching on match day is managing behavior—both yours and your athletes'. The two are closely connected.

Your Conduct

You very much influence your athletes' behavior before, during, and after a match. If you're up, your athletes are more likely to be up. If you're anxious, they'll notice, and the anxiety can be contagious. If you're negative, they'll respond with worry. If you're positive, they'll wrestle with more enjoyment. If you're constantly yelling instructions or commenting on mistakes and errors, it will be difficult for your athletes to concentrate. Instead, let athletes get into the flow of the match.

The focus should be on positive competition and on having fun. A coach who overorganizes everything and dominates matches from the bench is definitely not making the match fun.

So how should you conduct yourself on the bench? Here are a few pointers:

- Be calm, in control, and supportive of your athletes.
- Encourage athletes often, but instruct during matches only sparingly. Athletes should be focusing on their performance during a match, not on instructions shouted from the bench.
- If you need to instruct an athlete, do so when you're both on the bench, in an unobtrusive manner. Never yell at athletes for making a mistake. Instead, briefly demonstrate or remind them of the correct technique and encourage them.

Remember, you're not competing for an Olympic gold medal! At this level, wrestling competitions are designed to help athletes develop their skills and themselves—and to have fun. So coach at matches in a manner that helps your athletes grow as athletes and people and enjoy themselves.

Athletes' Conduct

You're responsible for keeping your athletes under control. Do so by setting a good example and by disciplining when necessary. Set team rules of good behavior. If athletes attempt to cheat, fight, argue, badger, yell disparaging remarks, and the like, it is your responsibility to correct the misbehavior. Consider team rules in these areas of match conduct:

- Athletes' language
- Athletes' behavior
- Interactions with officials

⊙ Discipline for misbehavior

⊙ Dress code for competitions

Athletes' Physical Safety

We devoted all of chapter 3 to discussing how to provide for athletes' safety, but it's worth noting here that safety during matches can be affected by how officials are calling the rules. If they aren't calling rules correctly, and this risks injury to your athletes, you must intervene. Voice your concern in a respectful manner and in a way that places the emphasis where it should be: on the athletes' safety. One of the officials' main responsibilities is to provide for athletes' safety; you are not adversaries here. Don't hesitate to address an issue of safety with an official when the need arises.

Athletes' Psychological Welfare

Athletes often attach their self-worth to winning and losing. This idea is fueled by coaches, parents, peers, and society, who place great emphasis on winning. Athletes become anxious when they're uncertain if they can meet the expectations of others or of themselves.

If you place too much importance on the match or cause your athletes to doubt their abilities, they will become anxious about the outcome and their performance. If your athletes look uptight and anxious during a match, find ways to reduce both the uncertainties about how their performance will be evaluated and the importance they are attaching to the competition. Help athletes focus on realistic personal goals—goals that are reachable and measurable and that will help them improve their performance. Another way to reduce anxiety on match day is to stay away from emotional prematch pep talks. We provided guidance earlier in what to address before the competition.

When coaching during matches, remember that the most important outcome is athletes' enhanced self-worth. Keep that firmly in mind, and strive to make every coaching decision promote your athletes' self-worth.

Opponents and Officials

Respect opponents and officials. Without them, you wouldn't have a competition. Officials help provide a fair and safe experience for athletes and, as appropriate, help them learn about wrestling. Opponents provide opportunities for your team to test itself, improve, and excel.

You and your team should show respect for opponents by giving your best efforts. You owe them this. Showing respect doesn't necessarily mean being "nice" to your opponents, though it does mean being civil.

Don't allow your athletes to "trash talk" or taunt an opponent. Such behavior is disrespectful to the spirit of the competition and to the opponent. Immediately remove an athlete from a match if he or she disobeys your orders in this area.

Remember that officials are quite often teenagers—in many cases not much older than the athletes themselves. The level of officiating should be commensurate with the level of play. In other words, don't expect perfection from officials any more than you do from your own athletes. Keep in mind that the officials are there to help athletes learn the rules and skills, too.

After the Match

When the match is over, join your team in congratulating the coaches and athletes of the opposing team; then be sure to thank the officials. Check on any injuries athletes sustained and let athletes know how to care for them. Be prepared to speak with the officials about any problems that occurred during the match. Then hold a brief team circle, as explained in a moment, to ensure that your athletes are on an even keel, whether they won or lost.

Winning With Class, Losing With Dignity

When celebrating a victory, make sure your team does so in a way that doesn't show disrespect for the opponents. It's fine and appropriate to be happy and celebrate a win, but don't allow your athletes to taunt the opponents or boast about their victory. Keep winning in perspective. Winning and losing are a part of life, not just a part of sport. If athletes can handle both equally well, they'll be successful in whatever they do.

Athletes are competitors, and competitors will be disappointed in defeat. If your team has made a winning effort, let them know that. After a loss, help them keep their chins up and maintain a positive attitude that will carry over into the next practice and match.

Team Circle

If your athletes have performed well in a match, compliment them and congratulate them immediately afterward. Tell them specifically what they did well, whether they won or lost. This will reinforce their desire to repeat their good performances.

Don't criticize individual athletes for poor performances in front of teammates. Help athletes improve their skills, but do so in the next practice, not immediately after a match.

The postgame team circle isn't the time to go over tactical problems and adjustments. The athletes are either so happy after a win or so dejected after a loss that they won't absorb much tactical information immediately afterwards. Your first concern should be your athletes' attitudes and mental well-being. You don't want them to be too high after a win or too low after a loss. This is the time you can be most influential in keeping the outcome in perspective and keeping them on an even keel.

Finally, make sure your athletes have transportation home. Be the last one to leave in order to help if transportation falls through and to ensure full supervision of athletes before they leave.

Rules and Equipment

This is where we'll introduce you to some of the basic rules of wrestling. We won't try to cover all the rules of the game, but rather we'll give you what you need to work with players who are 8 to 14 years old. We'll give you information on how kids benefit from wrestling, what the basic rules are, and the equipment needed. We'll then explain the three types of wrestling and describe the weight classes, match structure, scoring, and tournament setup for each. You will also find the referee signals at the end of the chapter.

Wrestling is the oldest form of recreational combat, arguably the oldest sport, with roots traced back thousands of years. Archaeologists have discovered ancient carvings and drawings in Africa, Europe, and Asia showing wrestlers in holds and positions of leverage. Many of these holds and maneuvers are the same as those you will be teaching your kids.

How Do Kids Benefit From Wrestling?

Wrestling is a popular sport for kids. One particularly attractive feature is that wrestlers are matched up according to weight and age. This allows youngsters too small to compete in other sports to face opponents of approximately the same size and to compete in age-group programs from the preteens through adulthood. The benefits youngsters derive from wrestling are

- physical development,
- nutritional awareness, and
- psychosocial growth.

Physical Development

Good wrestlers at any level are in top physical condition. Any youngster who participates on a club or school team for a reasonable length of time stands to benefit physically and show greater

- flexibility,
- coordination,
- endurance,
- body awareness, and
- strength.

Admittedly, youngsters can get many of these benefits by participating in other sports. But in many sports, kids spend their time learning and trying to master skills used in that sport alone, such as hitting a baseball or dribbling a basketball. In contrast, wrestling promotes the learning of many general movement skills that can help youngsters succeed not only in wrestling but also in other activities.

Nutritional Awareness

Because wrestlers are grouped by weight as well as by age, youngsters are likely to develop good nutritional habits at an early age (see chapter 8). As a group, young wrestlers generally will be much more aware of nutrition than others their age. And wrestling's emphasis on both general conditioning and proper nutrition usually helps youngsters achieve the weight and percentage of body fat that is healthiest for them.

It won't happen automatically, however, so you must be prepared to provide them the nutritional guidance they need.

Psychosocial Growth

When youngsters participate in organized wrestling programs, they stand to benefit psychologically and socially from the

⊙ increased self-responsibility,

⊙ sense of achievement,

⊙ added self-confidence,

⊙ new friends, and

⊙ exposure to new experiences.

When a wrestler steps onto the mat to face an opponent, his ability to perform effectively depends on his mind as well as his body. That's because this is a sport of action and reaction, and there simply isn't enough time for a wrestler to wait for instructions from his coach. And, because every opponent is slightly different, no two matches are ever alike. In short, wrestlers learn to think on their feet and gain confidence to move forward without counsel.

Youngsters can feel a real sense of accomplishment when they win. What's just as important, however, is that they learn to accept responsibility for their losses. In that regard, wrestling helps kids mature. As a coach, you play a major role in enabling them to learn and benefit from their experiences.

Underachievers, through wrestling, might gain the added self-confidence they need to be more successful in other aspects of their lives. Loners may gain new friends and become more adept at handling different social experiences. Plus, every kid who wrestles can learn about setting reasonable goals and working to achieve them, and about teamwork and fair play.

Without question, young wrestlers will encounter a variety of new situations. In practices, at matches, or on the road for tournaments, youngsters will be soaking in first-time experiences at every turn. They'll also be meeting new acquaintances along the way. You can help expand their horizons and social network by exposing them to as many positive opportunities and individuals as possible.

Now, before we turn to the rules of wrestling, let's look at some terms commonly used in wrestling.

Terms to Know

Wrestling has its own vocabulary. Being familiar with common terms will make your job easier. Pages 78–85 demonstrate official signals used in wrestling.

Breakdown: From the down position, a wrestler who is on top is expected to flatten the bottom wrestler out and turn him for a pin in folkstyle wrestling. This process is known as "breaking him down." Some common breakdowns are the tight-waist, arm chop, spiral ride, and ankle picks. (In freestyle and Greco-Roman a wrestler on the bottom is expected to stall, keeping his chest to the mat and resisting exposure or turns until the referee returns the wrestlers to their feet.)

Chicken wing: A common pinning or riding hold. A wrestler will chop his opponent's arm and work to overhook the arm. A wrestler who can hold this overhook and get his hand across his opponent's back has established a chicken wing.

Choice: In folkstyle wrestling each wrestler chooses the starting position for one period. Wrestlers start the first period from the neutral position. Prior to the second period, the referee flips a coin to determine who has first choice. The wrestler with the first choice can choose top, bottom, or neutral as the starting position, or he can defer his choice to the third period. As a point of strategy, wrestlers most commonly choose the bottom position because as wrestlers advance in skill, they feel escapes are easy to come by.

Cradle: This is another pinning hold that wrestlers learn early in their careers. A wrestler who can lock his hands over his opponent's head while squeezing the opponent's leg to the opponent's head has gained control of a cradle. He would be said to have "locked up a cradle."

Decision: This is a victory determined by points scored for takedowns, escapes, reversals, near falls, and in some instances such as college matches, time advantage.

Default: This is the outcome of a match when one wrestler is injured and unable to wrestle or to continue wrestling.

Disqualification: This is a match in which a wrestler is declared the loser because he has violated the rules.

Down position: In the down position a wrestler will start with his hands in front of the starting line and his knees behind. The top wrestler will assume the control position by grasping the opponent's elbow with one hand and the naval or midsection with the other hand. In folkstyle wrestling a wrestler can choose to start a period from the down position. If action travels out of bounds, a wrestler who is under the control of his opponent will restart action from the down position.

Escape: An escape is getting away from the opponent and gaining a neutral position.

Fall: The fall is the ultimate objective and occurs when one wrestler pins his opponent's shoulders to the mat for a specified time, ending the match.

Forfeit: This is the outcome of a match in which one wrestler fails to appear.

Front headlock: This move is often used as a counter to an opponent's shot (or attempt at a takedown). It involves the wrestler sprawling his legs back and trapping an opponent's head under his chest while locking around the opponent's arm. Once a front headlock is controlled, a wrestler will try to go behind his opponent for a takedown.

Granby: A granby is a complex rolling maneuver often used from the bottom position. The wrestler rolls from the bottom position and catches control of the opponent's arm and leg to establish control, then takes the opponent directly to his back. From the bottom position, a granby can quickly score a wrestler five points. A skilled wrestler can hit a granby as an opponent goes behind for a takedown or hit it from his feet if an opponent slips behind him.

Half-nelson: This is the simplest of pinning combinations. A wrestler will reach under an opponent's arm from behind and grab the back of the opponent's head. He then will pry the arm up while driving into the opponent chest to chest to get near-fall points.

Illegal hold: Some types of holds or techniques are illegal in wrestling. Wrestlers who use an illegal maneuver are penalized a point. Common illegal holds include a full-nelson, illegal headlocks in which the wrestler doesn't encircle an arm, or locking hands around an opponent's waist when the wrestler is on top or in control of his opponent. Here is a description of an illegal hold: "He would have won the match, but he 'locked his hands' and gave the opponent a point for the victory."

Intentional release: A wrestler who is very good at takedowns or who needs to catch up with his opponent in points may intentionally release an opponent, giving him an escape point. The wrestler then will try to score a takedown for two points, thus trading the opponent's one point for the release for a takedown that is (hopefully) worth two points. Coaches often teach this legal tactic, known as "cutting him." Here's a description of its use: "My wrestler cut him and took him down for two points to win the match in the last seconds."

Leg-ride: An advanced wrestler in the top position may have learned to use his legs in a leg-ride. This is also called the grapevine position. Wrapping a leg tightly around an opponent's leg can lead to pinning combinations such as a power half or guillotine. A leg-ride also is an effective way to ride out an opponent: "He put the legs in on him and turned him."

Major decision: This is a decision by a specified margin of points in folkstyle wrestling.

Near fall: Wrestlers score near-fall points (also known as back points) by holding their opponent's shoulders in a danger (exposed) position on the opponent's back. Once the opponent's shoulders break a 90-degree angle, the referee will begin to count near fall. If the referee counts to two while the shoulders are exposed, it is worth two points. If the referee counts to five while the shoulders are exposed, it is worth three points.

Pin: If a wrestler can pin an opponent's shoulder/scapula to the mat for a two count, this is a fall and the match is terminated.

Pummel: A wrestler who can fight through an opponent's arms or upper body is said to pummel into position. Pummeling is the process of establishing a tieup, such as an underhook, by digging, squeezing, and fighting for position.

Reversal: Exchanging control from the bottom to the top position. Common reversals are: the switch, the granby and the stepover.

Ride: A wrestler who is on top is said to be riding his opponent while working for a breakdown and turn to a pin. Late in a match a wrestler might be ahead by a point with 10 seconds left in the match. That wrestler needs to ride out the opponent and prevent him from getting an escape or reversal for one or two points. "Ride him out," the coach would be urging from the corner.

Setup: Strategies used by a wrestler to finesse his opponent out of position so that the wrestler can initiate a score. From the neutral position a wrestler might set up the opponent by popping the opponent's arms up or dragging them across his body.

Shoot or shot: When wrestlers work for a takedown, they work on attacks, also known as shots. A wrestler will shoot on his opponent in a variety of ways with different takedowns such as a sweep single, an inside-step hi-c, a low single, or an outside-step single.

Sprawl: When a wrestler is shot on or attacked by his opponent, the reaction of throwing the legs back to counter the shot is a sprawl. From the sprawl wrestlers learn counterattacks such as snapping and spinning behind or locking up a front headlock to a front quarternelson.

Stalling/passivity: In a match one wrestler might consistently be trying to slow the pace of the match. This can happen when a wrestler is tired or is trying to protect a lead. The referee can warn or call a wrestler for stalling. A second stalling call earns his opponent a point. A wrestler who is called for passivity in the international styles of freestyle or Greco-Roman wrestling is placed in the down position.

Stance: Wrestlers begin the match in a wrestling stance. Basically there are two types of stance: a square stance, in which a wrestler's feet are wide below the shoulders, and a stagger stance, in which one foot is place in a forward or stride position.

Standup: The basic way a wrestler escapes from an opponent is a standup. To successfully escape, a wrestler must clear his arms and step out while pressuring back into the top wrestler. Once the wrestler gets to his feet, he must maintain his balance and peel his opponent's hands off to break the lock so that he can turn and face his opponent. All of this happens while the top wrestler is aggressively working to return him to the mat.

Switch: From the bottom position wrestlers can score by escaping their opponent's grasp (worth one point) or reversing their opponent's control (worth two points). Commonly the first reversal technique taught to wrestlers is the switch. A switch involve clearing the arms, sitting to a hip, and reaching back to the opponent's leg to a go-behind position.

Takedown: A maneuver to establish control over an opponent from an open position in which neither wrestler has control of the other. A takedown is worth two points in folkstyle wrestling. In freestyle and Greco-Roman wrestling, a takedown may be worth one, two, three, or five points, depending on the amplitude of the takedown.

Technical fall: This is a match that ends when a certain point spread is reached.

Throw: A wrestler who advances in skill can learn ways to take an opponent from his feet quickly to his back. This is known as throwing an opponent. Common throws include headlocks, bodylocks, and arm spins: "He threw him in a bodylock and stuck (pinned) him."

Tieup: From the neutral position, opponents contact each other in basic tieups. Some of the common tieups include underhooks, wrist ties, head ties, and elbow ties.

Time advantage: In collegiate wrestling only, a credit for the net time one wrestler spends in control of the other. Also called riding time.

Whizzer: A whizzer is a counter to a shot. The wrestler wraps his arm over his opponent's arm while he is being attacked. The wrap of the arm is known as a whizzer and is used to pull an opponent off of his attack.

Rules

Wrestling is not a highly complex sport. But because of the physical contact and exertion inherent in it, you must fully inform your wrestlers of the rules that do exist and make sure that they abide by them. Knowledge of the rules is also necessary to teach maneuvers and strategy properly.

Matches

All wrestling matches begin with the two wrestlers on their feet, facing each other in a neutral position, with no advantage to either one. The duration of a match is specified according to the wrestling style and the age group involved. It can be cut short by a fall; technical fall; injury; forfeit (failure to appear); or by disqualification for misconduct, stalling, or any other violation of the rules the referee believes warrants it. Although wrestling is a "combat" sport, any hold or maneuver applied with the intent to injure the opponent is prohibited. A referee, timekeeper, and scorekeeper are necessary to conduct an official match.

Wrestling has two principal forms of competition:

◉ Dual meets between two teams, which match a wrestler from each team in each of several weight classes

◉ Tournaments, in which several teams or several wrestlers enter in each weight class; team competition may or may not be involved.

Classification Systems

The wrestlers are matched up by weight and by age or grade in school. A weigh-in is held before the competition; the wrestlers' body weights must be within certain limits specified for their age group and style of competition. The "unlimited" weight class no longer exists, so even the heaviest wrestlers must stay within established limits.

Equipment

Soft shoes with flat soles are required. The shoes may not have metal eyelets, and the rigid tips of shoelaces must be cut off. The one-piece uniform is called a singlet, under which the wrestler must wear an athletic supporter or underbrief. Protective headgear is required in folkstyle competition and is encouraged for young athletes in Olympic-style competition.

Wrestling takes place on a mat about an inch and a half thick and some 25 to 30 feet across. The wrestling area is almost always circular. Modern mats are made of a foam-core plastic that is easily cleaned and has great cushioning capacity.

Wrestling Styles

Many different wrestling styles are found around the world, including schwingen in Switzerland; glima in Iceland; sumo in Japan; and tchidaoba, kokh, gulech, and kurach in various republics of the former Soviet Union. Each style has different rules, but all have virtually the same objective: to take the opponent from his feet to the ground, to turn him over (or to throw him on his back), and to hold his shoulders down.

Three types of wrestling are recognized and practiced in the United States, and as a club or school coach, you probably will be involved in all three: folkstyle, freestyle, and Greco-Roman. High school and college wrestlers engage in folkstyle competitions, which emphasize taking an opponent down and controlling him on the mat.

Freestyle and Greco-Roman are the two international styles used in the modern Olympic Games. Freestyle is similar to folkstyle, although it places less emphasis on control and more on turning the opponent's back toward the mat. The Greco-Roman style, which originated in Europe during the Napoleonic era, prohibits grasping the opponent's legs or using the legs to trip or hold the opponent. Because the legs can't be used to attack or defend, the Greco-Roman style often produces spectacular lifts and throws.

Folkstyle

In this section we will address the basic rules of scholastic wrestling. Collegiate rules vary somewhat, primarily in the number and limits on weight classes, the length of matches, and whether or not a minute of time advantage is worth a point.

Weight Classes

The high school level has 13 or 14 folkstyle weight classifications.

13 to 14 Folkstyle Weight Classification (pounds)

up to 103	up to 145
up to 112	up to 152
up to 119	up to 160
up to 125	up to 171
up to 130	up to 189
up to 135	up to 215 (optional)
up to 140	up to 275

The youth (pre-high school) level offers lower weight classes to accommodate very small wrestlers. For example, the 13-to-14 age group has a lower limit of 70 pounds; 11- to 12-year-olds start as low as 60 pounds; and kids 9 to 10 can weigh as little as 50 pounds.

Although weight classes differ by age, the system for entering athletes into competitions is the same for all levels. In a dual meet, each team may enter one wrestler in each weight class. The same is true for most tournaments. However, in open tournaments, a school or club may enter as many wrestlers as it wishes, and individuals can enter on their own.

Match Structure

The match is divided into three periods. The first period starts with both wrestlers standing. The second and third periods can start with both wrestlers down on the mat, one in a position of advantage, or with the wrestlers on their feet in a neutral position. A coin toss determines which wrestler gets the choice of position. The first period in a college match is 3 minutes long and the second and third periods are 2 minutes each. High school matches follow the same format, but have 2-minute periods. Pre-high school matches have 1-minute (or shorter) periods.

Scoring

Depending on the starting position for each period, the wrestlers try to score takedowns, escapes, reversals, and near falls to control their opponents on the mat, to turn them over, and then to pin their shoulders for a fall. The successful execution of these maneuvers is rewarded with match points.

To understand how the various maneuvers and penalties are scored, see table 7.1.

Table 7.1

Maneuver	Penalty
Takedown	2 points
Escape	1 point
Reversal	2 points
Near fall	2 or 3 points (depending on the length of time a wrestler is held on his back)

A fall is called when an opponent's shoulders are pinned to the mat and held for 2 seconds (high school and college). If neither wrestler scores a fall, the winner is determined by the number of points earned. A victory by eight or more points is a major decision. A margin of 15 points is a technical fall and ends the match.

In a dual meet, the performance of each wrestler determines whether his team receives points and how many. A decision is worth three points; a major decision, four; a technical fall, five; and a fall, six. The loser receives no points. Winning by injury default, forfeit, or disqualification counts the same as a fall.

Tournaments

In a tournament, the brackets on which wrestlers' names appear determine the order of pairing. Winners advance to face other winners until one becomes champion. Top-rated wrestlers are oftentimes placed in opposite brackets (a practice called seeding) so that they will not be paired against each other until the final matches. Almost all tournaments have a consolation or double-elimination format, so that a wrestler who has lost only once still has an opportunity to place in the standings.

It is customary to award the successful wrestlers some token of achievement, traditionally medals or ribbons for first, second, and third places. In large tournaments, additional places are often recognized. In team competition, teams receive points for the placings of their individuals and bonus points when their wrestlers win by falls, technical falls, or major decisions. Winning teams receive trophies.

Freestyle

Whereas folkstyle is officiated by one referee, freestyle matches require three officials, two of whom must agree on any ruling. This international style is much faster and more spectacular than folkstyle.

Weight Classes

Freestyle wrestling also has 8 weight classes for adult competition. The lightest weight category is up to 119 pounds, whereas the upper limit on the heaviest class is 286 pounds.

As in folkstyle, youth competition offers more weight classes to choose from, and the limits are scaled to allow very small wrestlers to compete against others their size.

Match Structure

A match is one continuous period of 3 minutes (adult and high school), 2 minutes (ages 11 to 14), or 1.5 minutes (10 and under). Wrestlers start the competition on their feet.

This international style requires wrestlers to be aggressive and to be willing to take risks in order to score. Officials are quick to penalize wrestlers for stalling, intentionally going out of bounds, or otherwise limiting the action.

Scoring

The scoring system used in freestyle is not quite as clear-cut as that used in folkstyle. Points are awarded for the spectacular nature of some maneuvers and not just for the maneuver itself. The greater the risk and the more advanced the technique, the more points it earns. Points tend to be scored much more quickly in freestyle than in folkstyle.

Here is a breakdown of the scoring used in this wrestling style:

Takedown   1 to 5 points

Taking the opponent to the mat under control is worth one point. Taking him from his feet and then to his back scores two points. Taking him from his feet directly to his back scores three points. But if a wrestler takes the opponent from his feet to his back with a spectacular, high-arching throw, he receives five points.

Escape   1 point

In freestyle an escape point can be earned if the top wrestler locks his hands around the waist of his opponent. If the bottom man breaks the lock and the top man continues the attack then an escape point can be given.

Reversal   1 point

A reversal in freestyle, as in folkstyle is an exchange of control, when the wrestler underneath gains the top position.

Exposure   2 points
Exposure   1 point (if the opponent travels hand to hand across his back)

Exposure is freestyle's equivalent of the near fall and is defined as turning the opponent's back past a 90-degree vertical line with the mat, his head, shoulder, or elbow touching the mat. The exposure can be instantaneous (like a quick roll across the back). If the exposure is the result of a lift and throw, it can be awarded 3 or 5 points. A fall is called in about half a second.

Control in the danger position 1 point

If a wrestler holds an opponent in an exposed position on his back for the count of five, he is awarded an additional exposure point for control in the danger or nearfall position.

Kids' wrestling has its own modifications of the international rules. Certain maneuvers with a high risk of injury, such as the most spectacular lifts and throws, are prohibited in youth competition. A fall must be controlled and held for 2 seconds so that an inexperienced youngster is less likely to pin himself by mistakenly rolling across his own shoulders.

Freestyle dual meets are held between clubs, schools, and even countries. Team points are awarded differently, too:

Fall   4 points

A technical fall (10-point margin) or an injury default, forfeit, or disqualification is considered equal to a fall and also scores four points.

| Superior decision | 3.5 points for a victory by a margin of 12 to 14 points |
| Decision | 3 points for a victory by a margin of 9 points or less |

If a losing wrestler scores at least one point during his bout, his team is awarded either one point (decision) or half a point (superior decision). A wrestler who loses by a fall or by a shutout does not earn any points for his team. A draw is not allowed. If a match ends in a tie, the wrestlers go directly into sudden-death overtime, with the first point winning the match.

Tournaments

Freestyle tournaments place the wrestlers' names on a chart by the drawing of numbers, rather than seeding. The contestants are divided into two groups, or pools. Preliminary rounds take place until all but three wrestlers in each pool have been eliminated by a second defeat. Those three compete against each other to determine placing within their group.

The winners of the two groups compete in the finals for first and second places. The runners-up in the groups wrestle for third and fourth places, and so on. Team awards are also presented.

Greco-Roman

Greco-Roman rules are the same as those for freestyle, with two exceptions. A Greco-Roman wrestler is not allowed to attack his opponent's legs, nor is he permitted to use his own legs to trip, lift, or execute other holds (including defensive holds). Refer to the freestyle section for weight classes, match structure, scoring, and the tournament system used in Greco-Roman wrestling.

What Style to Teach?

As a youth coach you will concentrate on teaching the basic skills, but the style of wrestling your athletes compete in will dictate some of the techniques, holds, and maneuvers you teach.

In both folkstyle and freestyle, the most important techniques are those that take the opponent to the mat. Single-leg and double-leg takedowns, the fireman's carry, arm drag, duck-under, heel pick, and inside trip are maneuvers to get the opponent off his feet and down to the mat. Of course, opposing coaches will be teaching the same things, so your wrestlers will need to learn defenses and counters against these techniques.

Sometimes the opponents will gain an advantage or score first, so your folkstyle wrestlers will have to know how to escape or score a reversal. The more common folkstyle techniques of sitout, standup, stepover, shoulder roll, and switch are seldom used in freestyle because they put the wrestler at risk of exposure with minimum potential for reward. However, some Olympic champions have relied on their past folkstyle experience to reverse for a victory.

Standard techniques for turning the opponent over, such as the half-nelson, arm bar, and cradle, are fundamental moves in both folkstyle and freestyle. Eventually your wrestlers should learn a couple of "big" moves (e.g., a throw) to attempt when they need a bunch of points in a hurry at the end of a losing match.

Don't bother with exposure moves such as the crotch lift and gut wrench during the folkstyle season because wrestlers usually can't score with these moves under folkstyle rules. If your team is learning Greco-Roman, don't spend time on single-leg and double-leg takedowns, trips, or other techniques that are prohibited by the rules. Instead, teach duck-unders, arm throws, lifts, and rolls through a bridge (gut wrench).

Every technique or maneuver you teach should include the stages of setup, execution, and follow-through. Don't forget the methods of defense and counterattack that have been developed specifically for each offensive move.

Exposing Wrestlers to All Styles

The transition from folkstyle to the international styles won't be difficult for a fundamentally sound wrestler. In fact, American wrestlers who go on to compete in world events are noted for being particularly well-conditioned, well-disciplined athletes. This conditioning and discipline result partially from the demands of folkstyle, in which a wrestler must learn how to dominate, control, and wear down an opponent.

Folkstyle wrestlers can also benefit from international style competition. The daring approach required in freestyle and Greco-Roman challenges wrestlers to add new dimensions to their technical skills.

a Stop the match

b Time-out

c Start the injury clock

d Stop the injury clock

Figure 7.1 Referee signals

e   Neutral position

f   No control

Figure 7.1   *(continued)*

g   Out of bounds

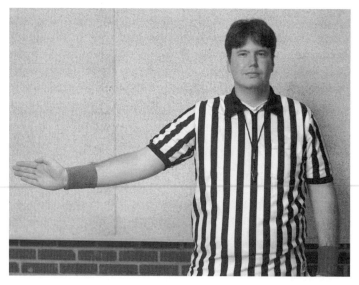

h   Wrestler in control—right or left hand

Figure 7.1   *(continued)*

i   Defer choice

j   Potentially dangerous move—right or left hand

k   Stalemate

Figure 7.1 *(continued)*

l   Caution for false start and incorrect starting position

m   Stalling—left or right hand

n   Interlocking hands or grasping clothing

Figure 7.1   *(continued)*

o Reversal

p Technical violation

q Illegal hold or unnecessary roughness

r Near-fall

Figure 7.1 *(continued)*

s Awarding points

t Unsportsmanlike conduct—right hand (green), left hand (red)

Figure 7.1 *(continued)*

 u Flagrant misconduct

Figure 7.1 *(continued)*

Getting Wrestlers in Shape

The good news is that wrestling encourages top physical conditioning. The bad news is that some wrestling coaches encourage harmful weight loss that is dangerous to a young athlete's health. The best news is that the bad news doesn't have to happen.

Because of its weight classification system and the amount of physical contact, no other sport creates as much weight awareness among athletes as wrestling. Unfortunately, too much weight sensitivity may result in unhealthy dietary behavior. This chapter will describe how you can help your wrestlers manage their weight effectively.

Nutrition, physical conditioning, and weight control are part of an athlete's total fitness package. However, you do not need to be a nutritionist, exercise physiologist, or dietician to provide your athletes the basic information and activities they need to get, and stay, in shape. Simply read this chapter and a few of the many fitness and health books available through ASEP and USA Wrestling, and you'll be prepared to advise and direct your wrestlers responsibly.

87

What Fitness Components Should Wrestlers Develop?

No athlete, particularly a wrestler, can afford to develop one part of the body or one component of physical fitness at the expense of another. The most successful wrestlers develop the following fitness components:

- Flexibility
- Endurance
- Strength
- Speed
- Balance

Flexibility

Adequate range of motion at all body joints is a must for wrestling participation. Muscles that are tight and restrict movement not only limit performance, but also represent an injury waiting to happen!

So, from the very first practice session to the very last meet, emphasize the importance of proper warm-up to your wrestlers. Each muscle group should be stimulated and lengthened. Stretches should be to the point of slight discomfort, then held in that position for several counts.

Controlled stretching is good for loosening tight muscles and making the body more flexible.

Each muscle group should be stretched at least three times, with a period of relaxation between stretches. If a wrestler's particular muscle group fails to loosen up after initial stretching, he should use it in a brief period of light activity, then attempt to stretch it out again.

The cool-down also is essential for flexibility. After practices and matches, have your wrestlers take at least 5 minutes to stretch the muscles they used. They'll be less tight before the next workout and experience less muscle soreness.

Endurance

As much as a wrestler needs to have heart on the mat to win, he also needs to condition his heart long before the match begins. A strong, well-conditioned cardiovascular system (heart and blood vessels) will enable his body to receive more oxygen and a higher volume of blood with every pump of the heart. It will also allow the wrestler to sustain a high level of exertion for a long time. Obviously, such cardiovascular conditioning will enhance both the youngster's health and his wrestling performance.

An excellent way to strengthen the cardiovascular system is to put it under controlled stress through progressively more intense aerobic exercise, which promotes the intake of oxygen. Most individuals prefer running, but cycling, calisthenics, circuit weight training, and aerobic dance are effective alternatives.

Cardiovascular benefits from such activities are produced when the athlete's heart rate remains at about 70 percent of its maximum for

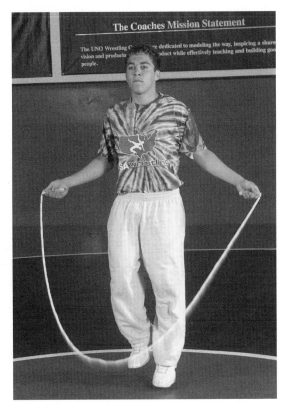

Jumping rope is an excellent way to improve cardiovascular fitness.

at least 25 minutes. To calculate the optimum heart rate, subtract the athlete's age in years from 220, then multiply by 70 percent. Thus, a 12-year-old who sustains a heart rate of 145 beats per minute for half an hour would benefit aerobically from the workout. The heart rate "target zone" is 60–90 percent of maximum. Wrestlers must engage in such exercise sessions at least three times a week to experience cardiovascular benefits.

Strength

The development of muscular strength through resistance training is an important part of total body conditioning. But any such programs should be prepared by a qualified athletic trainer and tailored for the age group involved. Because lifting is one of the seven basic skills, we will discuss the fundamentals of lifting in chapter 9. Young wrestlers may get all the lifting they need during everyday practice. However, some may benefit from strengthening specific muscle groups.

The best conditioning tool, along with running, is wrestling practice and the vigorous physical activity involved in practicing skills, repetitions, and competition. If you structure your practices correctly, your wrestlers should get much of the resistance work they need through the lifting they do during practice and conditioning exercises.

Good wrestling requires total body conditioning through resistance training and aerobic activity.

Speed and Balance

Some coaches believe that fitness and performance components are gifts of nature—athletes either have them or they don't. Included in the list of skills of a "natural athlete" are the components of speed and balance.

So what do you do if your roster includes several slow-moving, stumbling wrestlers? Don't give up just yet! Many informed coaches and countless athletes can attest to the fact that speed and balance can be improved through proper training. Plyometrics—quick, explosive movements—are especially effective for wrestlers. So have your athletes routinely engage in practice activities that require them to move in short bursts. Because body position and footwork are keys to balance, include a variety of agility activities in your workouts (see a–d). You and your wrestlers will be surprised at the results.

a

Shadow wrestling that includes movements such as shots, level changes, and sprawls can increase speed and balance.

(continued)

(continued)

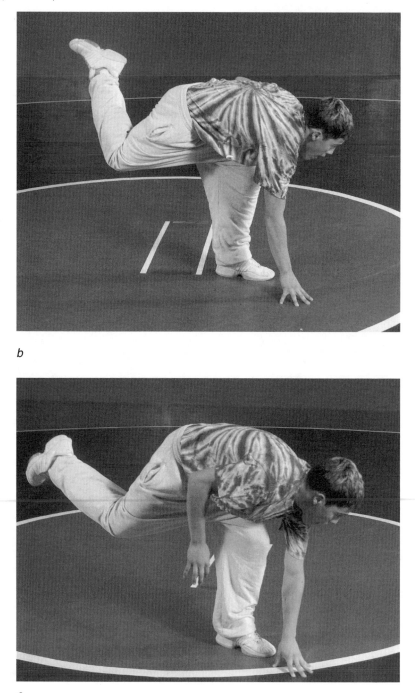

b

c

d

When Is Good Nutrition Important?

Just as a car runs best with a full tank of the proper fuel, an athlete's body will perform at its maximum only when it's filled with the right "nutritional fuel." For active athletes, that fuel consists of complex carbohydrates. During digestion, carbohydrate is broken down into glucose, an important energy source used by muscles during exercise.

A healthy, growing kid needs a balanced diet, including three meals a day in moderate portions. His diet should include foods from the four major food groups: dairy, meat, fruit and vegetable, and grain. The youngster should avoid high-fat, high-sugar foods and snacks such as potato chips, soft drinks, mayonnaise, candy bars, and ice cream, and emphasize instead foods that are rich in complex carbohydrates, such as cereals, pasta, baked potatoes, and vegetables.

If you think nutrition starts and stops the week of the match, you're mistaken. Nutrition and hydration play important—and different—roles throughout the season. For our purposes, however, nutrition needs are greatest

⊙ throughout training and practice,

⊙ before and during competition, and

⊙ following competition.

Training and Practice

Throughout the season the young wrestler needs a regular diet that supplies energy to support him during his training and practice schedule. A well-balanced diet rich in complex carbohydrates is essential for supplying energy and building muscle glycogen levels. How many calories a wrestler needs depends on how many calories he burns each day. This isn't always easy to determine because the energy burned varies with body size, body composition, and the intensity and duration of workouts. You should consult an athletic trainer or a sports medicine physician to design a diet matched to the wrestler's specific caloric requirements.

Prematch Meal

Many wrestlers don't understand the exact role of the prematch meal because foods only increase muscle glycogen levels after 2 or 3 days. However, the prematch meal is important for increasing blood glucose and liver glycogen stores, energy sources used in the early stages of competition. If blood glucose levels are high at the start of the match, the wrestler will be able to compete longer before having to use muscle glycogen stores.

To avoid stomach upset, nausea, or a "stuffed" feeling, tell your wrestlers to eat a meal 3 to 4 hours before the match.

Advise them to avoid spicy, fatty foods. These are difficult to digest and may cause distress during the match. Also, discourage the intake of high-fat, high-protein foods such as steaks, hamburgers, french fries, chips, and mayonnaise.

Conversely, cereals, pasta, baked potatoes, and muffins are good carbohydrate sources that are easily digested. Vegetables and fruit juices are also good prematch foods, as are some dairy products such as low-fat yogurt, ice milk, and low-fat milk.

Postmatch Recovery

Because a wrestling match is continuous, a wrestler doesn't have a chance to replace body fluids during the competition itself. Since body fluids are lost by sweating, the wrestler should replace them by sipping water as soon as the bout is over in order to start the body's recovery period.

Recovering from the match is just as important as preparing for it, particularly in a tournament situation in which the wrestler has several matches in one day. Even with regular fluid breaks, large quantities of body water may be lost in the form of sweat. Moreover, muscle glycogen levels may be low, leaving the wrestler feeling weak and exhausted. Now is the time to start the recovery process so that the wrestler can resume practice and competition with renewed energy and endurance. Encourage your wrestlers to continue rehydrating for several hours after the match and to eat foods rich in carbohydrates to speed the rate of glycogen recovery.

What About Making Weight?

Wrestling is a sport for individuals of all shapes and sizes. This is one of our sport's greatest assets. However, the very weight-class system that allows both the big athlete and the little athlete to achieve success also lends itself to abuse by wrestlers, coaches, and parents. Specifically, weight cutting and the manipulation of body fluids is harmful to both the health of the individual and the reputation of the sport.

In striving for maximum performance, wrestlers often overlook two key areas: nutrition and hydration. To lose unwanted pounds, they starve and dehydrate themselves, or they "bulk up" by eating and drinking large quantities to gain weight. Both dietary practices reduce strength and endurance.

The sad part of the story is that such behavior often is condoned, even encouraged, by adults who have lost perspective. The coach may be looking at an empty weight class in his lineup and thinking, "Wouldn't it be great if we could cut Billy down 10 pounds and have a bigger, stronger wrestler in that weight?" But it's like cramming a size 9 foot into a size 7 shoe. It may be bigger, but it's not necessarily stronger, and it's going to hurt!

Parents too can pressure their kids to "succeed" by cutting weight. This pressure is oftentimes a product of a parent's ego and is something you should address in a preseason meeting.

We know that a competitive athlete should be hungry to perform and to win, but a young wrestler who is constantly hungry for food is likely to be unhappy and less effective. His discontent may well spread to his studies and to his social life. Both his physical and emotional health could be in danger.

Choosing a Proper Weight Class

Weight classes increase at intervals of as little as 5, 6, or 7 pounds, depending on the wrestling style. Because of this, many wrestlers are tempted to cut weight and compete against smaller opponents. Discourage such weight cutting and help your athletes find the proper weight class. Your wrestlers' health, happiness, and success are at stake.

For example, a high school wrestler who weighs 150 pounds may be caught between two weight classes. He can either drop 5 pounds and compete at 145 or compete under the 152-pound ceiling—perhaps against larger opponents who have dropped their own weight from 160 or more. The inclination of most wrestlers (and their coaches) in such situations is to embark immediately on a weight-loss program. Such a decision may cost the wrestler on the mat and off. He might not be as effective at 145 as he was at 150. His coach might better have advised him to put on a few pounds of muscle than to take off needed weight.

Determining Optimal Body Weight

Before selecting a weight class, the wrestler and his coach should determine his optimal competitive weight. This optimal weight is neither his lowest possible weight nor the weight at which he can best make the lineup. It should be the wrestler's healthiest weight—the one at which he can perform most effectively without slowing his normal growth.

An accurate way to gauge optimal body weight is by the percentage of fat tissue in the body. This should be measured during the preseason medical examination by using skinfold calipers or hydrostatic (underwater) weighing. The physician then will recommend whether the body fat percentage should be reduced.

Obviously, the health and performance of a wrestler with 25 percent body fat would improve if his fat percentage were reduced. Body fat can be lowered by reducing caloric intake, by raising the level of activity, or by a combination of the two. But a young wrestler whose body fat is below 10 percent may be well advised to increase his caloric intake.

Any weight control program should start a couple of months before the official start of the wrestling season. If weight loss is appropriate, help your wrestler chart an 8-week program of increased activity and lowered caloric intake. Follow the standard dietary advice found in this chapter. Keep reminding the athlete that very fast weight reduction is not the answer. Although he may lose 3 pounds in a 24-hour period by fasting, two thirds of that stems from water loss and a depletion of vital energy supplies of glucose and glycogen. Two pounds a week is as fast as weight should be reduced.

Check That Excess Baggage

Explain to your athletes that excess baggage in the body is never the result of drinking too much water. When we eat too much, our bodies store the excess in fat. When we drink too much, our bodies simply eliminate whatever they cannot use. For this reason, young wrestlers should make a point of drinking several glasses of water every day. Encourage them to drink water occasionally instead of snacking; this will help curb their hunger and reduce the number of empty calories they are taking in.

Too many wrestlers try to squeeze into lower weight classes by constantly eliminating or restricting their water intake before weigh-in. This is just about the worst thing a wrestler can do. Whether water is eliminated quickly in a sauna, with the aid of a diuretic, or by restricting the intake of water, asking the body to function with a subnormal level of fluid is dangerous. Even when as much as 5 hours is allowed for rehydration after weigh-in, the balance between fluids and electrolytes cannot be completely reestablished; therefore, the wrestler remains dehydrated.

Studies by the American College of Sports Medicine clearly show that dehydration causes a loss of electrolytes, the electrical conductors that play an important role in maintaining the body's chemical balance. An electrolyte imbalance can diminish strength and coordination; slow reaction time; and affect heart, kidney, and neurological functioning. Such changes can impede normal growth and development and threaten youngsters' health.

Cut Out the Weight Cutting

Weight that comes off during training, conditioning, and by switching to a healthy, balanced diet is probably excess poundage that was detrimental to the athlete's health and wrestling performance. However, in youth wrestling any other weight should be maintained by wrestlers. At the high school level, there are regulations against dangerous weight-cutting practices. On the college scene, success is more a matter of weight control and weight management than weight cutting. The National Collegiate Athletic Association, for example, has taken a strong stand against radical dehydration and its inherent health hazards.

The focus of weight reduction must be on physical fitness. Exercise is important in expending calories and also in maintaining a proper diet. Therefore, encourage wrestlers to continue workouts during their weight reduction periods. If athletes must snack between meals, encourage them to choose fruit or vegetables rather than cookies or candy.

Finally, instruct and motivate your athletes to follow good nutritional practices every day, not just the day before a match. Praise and reward them for sticking to the program. Make clear to them that if they take shortcuts on their diets or any part of their conditioning programs, they can expect to suffer the consequences on the mat.

chapter **9**

Tactics and Skills

A s your athletes play games in practice, their experience in these games—and your subsequent discussions with them about their experience—will lead them to the tactics and skills they need to develop in order to succeed. In the games approach to teaching wrestling, tactics and skills go hand in hand.

In this chapter we'll provide information that will help you teach your athletes the Seven Basic Skills, suggest how to use them as a base for teaching specific maneuvers, and recommend a variety of games you can use to develop your wrestlers' abilities. Remember to use the IDEA approach to teaching skills—Introduce, Demonstrate, and Explain the skill, and Attend to players as they practice the skill. For a refresher on IDEA, see chapter 5. If you aren't familiar with wrestling skills, rent or purchase a video to see the skills performed. You may also find advanced books on skills helpful.

We provide information about only the basics of wrestling in this book. As your wrestlers advance in their wrestling skills, you'll need to advance in your knowledge as a coach. You can do so by learning from your experiences, by watching and talking with more experienced coaches, and by studying advanced resources. Many such resources are available from USA Wrestling and the American Sport Education Program.

What Are the Seven Basic Skills?

Mastery of the basic wrestling skills is essential to the proper execution of all holds and maneuvers. The skills are the building blocks on which all other instruction must be laid. The Seven Basic Skills lead to the development of specific techniques and maneuvers, in turn setting the stage for competition and strategy.

Good wrestlers have instinctively practiced sound fundamental skills for centuries. But don't leave your wrestlers' learning to chance. Teach them the Seven Basic Skills in a systematic manner.

- ⊙ Skill 1: Position
- ⊙ Skill 2: Motion
- ⊙ Skill 3: Changing levels
- ⊙ Skill 4: Penetration
- ⊙ Skill 5: Lifting
- ⊙ Skill 6: Back step
- ⊙ Skill 7: Back arch

Skill 1: Position

Call it stance, call it posture. By any term, proper body position—the ability of a wrestler to control specific parts of the body in relation to each other—is the first requirement for successful execution of any primary maneuver.

Your wrestler should assume a semisquatting position with knees slightly bent and feet approximately shoulder-width apart. This foot spread provides both a wide base of support for stability and good balance for quick motion. Instruct each wrestler to face the opponent directly, with the toes of both feet forming a plane with the chest. The other option is to have the wrestler face the opponent on an angle, with one foot in front of the other.

The key parts of the body and their proper relationships to one another are as follows:

- Knees—bent (flexed), never any farther in front of the body than the chest
- Chest—up and out, always over a vertical plane with the knee
- Hips—low, flexed, and over the supporting points on the mat
- Feet—shoulder-width apart and under the center of gravity
- Head—always up and above the shoulders
- Hands—held in front of the hips, palms down
- Elbows—flexed, held in close to the hips
- Back—straight

Wrestling has three fundamental positions (see figure 9.1a–c): (*a*) top and bottom position, in which the wrestler on top is in control; (*b*) stagger position, in which the feet are staggered apart; and (*c*) square position, in which the feet are square and the body is aligned in proportion to the feet.

a

Figure 9.1 (a) top and bottom positions, (b) stagger position, (c) square position.

(continued)

b

c

Figure 9.1 *(continued)*

Position Games

SWITCHERS

Goal

To reverse control of an opponent

Description

Place two wrestlers in any of the following positions:

- Down on all fours, side to side, facing toward each other's ankles. Each wrestler grasps with the inside arm and lifts the near foot of the opponent, wrapping at the shoelaces; or wrestlers can grasp the nearest thigh.
- Sitting side to side, face and legs extended beyond opponent's back. Each wrestler grabs lever control on the near thigh of his opponent; or wrestlers can do this from a standing or kneeling position.

At the start, each wrestler has the same control over the other. The goal is to scramble into control over the opponent. These are common positions that allow switches and reversals to be gained in wrestling matches.

WRESTLER'S HANDSHAKE

Goal

To learn motion in a stance with contact

Description

Two wrestlers lock by grabbing each other at the forearm, right arm to right arm or left to left. Once in this position, wrestlers should use good forearm control with a good stance and motion to go behind the opponent. The wrestlers should use their free arms to grab behind the defender and reach for the far hip.

BULLDOZER

Goal

To enhance breakdown skills

Description

One defender kneels with both legs on the mat, hands resting on the knees, and the laces of his shoes to the mat. He should be in an upright position. The bulldozer cannot lock his hands around the kneeling wrestler's waist. On the start, the bulldozer tries to flatten the defender to the mat. The defender's goal is to maintain the kneeling position and move to a standup.

To make the game harder:

- Have wrestlers grapple from the standing position, allowing the bulldozer to lock around the waist and return the defender to the mat.
- Teach the bottom man to peel hands and face the bulldozer.

CAGED UP

Goal

To learn to move and fight through contact

Description

Five or six participants stand hip to hip in a circle with their hands around one another's backs to form a cage around one wrestler. The cage can only shift left and right with the hips and legs, and participants must keep their arms intertwined. The wrestler in the cage must get in a good stance with motion and fight through the gaps of the cage to get out.

COILED SPRINGS

Goal

To learn the correct way to take an opponent down with a single leg and teach the defender how to fall to his belly and face a defender properly

Description

One wrestler controls a defender's single leg. The single leg is high and the attacker maintains a stance with the head up and in the defender's chest. The defender works on balancing and returning to a safe position quickly. The defender does not receive a control point.

The attacker changes levels and drives the opponent to the mat using his single leg control. Once the defender falls to the mat, the attacker continues to control the single leg and maintain his balance while standing over the defender. Without the help of the attacker, the defender springs back to the safe starting position. He must use his free leg and hands to coil up and spring back to his feet.

Variation

- This can be a timed process or race against two other wrestlers.
- Coaches can score the number of times a defender falls to his belly as opposed to his back; this teaches the goal of not giving up a takedown.

Skill 2: Motion

Power is the result of two factors: strength and mobility. A wrestler's strength is of little value if he is unable to move the various parts of the body explosively into or away from the opponent. Maximum potential for quick movement, and thus maximum power, can be attained only through proper body position.

The ability to move laterally depends on keeping the arms (hands) and legs (feet) free and the muscles flexed and ready to explode. An arm or a leg that has been straightened out or pinned to the wrestler's own body, to that of the opponent, or to the mat cannot be used until it has been brought back to a coiled position.

A wrestler must be able to move in a free and fluid manner, so coach your wrestlers to circle their opponents or move into or away from them (see figure 9.2a–d). Smooth movement is the result of constant readjustment of the feet with quick, short, choppy steps. A quick spin around a single point of support (i.e., pivoting on one foot) enhances fast, smooth movement. Demonstrate the practical value of learning footwork skills by pointing out to your wrestlers that one of the important finishes to a single-leg takedown depends on this type of smooth, pivoting motion. Once the opponent's leg has been secured, if he drives into your wrestler, a quick circular movement will split his base and set him down.

a

b

Figure 9.2 Circling your opponent.

c

d

Figure 9.2 *(continued)*

Position and Motion Games

BULL RIDING

Goal

To work on bottom position and movement

Description

Divide the group into pairs. Start with one partner in the down position pretending to be a bull and the other sitting on the "bull's" back near his hips, feet off the floor, pretending to be a cowboy. On the whistle, the bull starts spinning in either direction and changing direction. The cowboy must ride the bull for 10 seconds without putting his feet down or falling off; he can hang on to the bull. Award the cowboy a point for a successful ride; award the bull a point for knocking the cowboy off.

To make the game easier:
- Allow the cowboy to put his feet down.

To make the game harder:
- Do not allow the cowboy to hold on.

FOX TAILS

Goal

To work on neutral position and movement

Description

Divide the group into pairs. Have each wrestler hang a sock or short towel (a tail) from the back of his shorts, 4 to 6 inches out of the shorts. Each wrestler tries to pull his partner's tail off. Award a point each time a wrestler pulls a tail.

To make the game easier:
- Lengthen the tail.

To make the game harder:
- Shorten the tail.
- Allow wrestlers to use only one hand.

SPINNING BEAR

Goal

To give the defender practice facing an opponent from an unstable stance while the attacker practices scoring a go-behind

Description

One wrestler is in a bear crawl position with only his hands and feet on the mat. To start the contest, the attacker must keep his hands on the bear. The bear cannot grab the attacker or drop to his knees. Rather, the bear should keep his head up and move his feet and hands to keep the attacker in front of him for as long as possible. The attacker should spin behind the bear, but in doing so he must keep his hands on the bear.

Variation

⊙ This variation is known as the Tumbling Bear. The bear continually tries to face the opponent while his opponent tries to make him fall to his back.

CRACK THE WHIP

Goal

To teach wrestlers how to scramble and return to a correct stance

Description

One wrestler barely has control of his opponent's foot or heel. In a strong stance, the attacker holds the foot tightly but just with his hands, relatively high toward the chest. The defender's job is to "crack the whip" and escape the ankle control of the opponent and return to neutral stance. The defender is on one knee and must pull free from his opponent by kicking or relaxing his foot free from the attacker. The attacker can only hold the ankle.

To make the game harder:

⊙ Give the attacker more control farther up the defender's leg.

Skill 3: Changing Levels

The skill that must precede the successful execution of any move is the ability to change levels in relation to the opponent and to the mat. This skill, unfortunately, is the one most often overlooked in the development of a good wrestler.

Changing levels is nothing more than motion in a vertical plane. Although many wrestlers consider lowering or raising their heads as the equivalent of changing levels, it is the ability to raise and lower the hips while remaining in good position that is the key to the success of this vertical motion.

Teach your wrestlers that the only way to change levels is to bend at the knees—going to a low squat and keeping the head up (see figure 9.3a–d). Only after properly changing levels and getting the hips down can a wrestler successfully move into the opponent. When executing a duck-under, an appropriate tug or snap on the opponent's head enables the wrestler to go down and immediately pop up behind him. Bending at the waist, however, leaves the wrestler vulnerable to a snapdown, arm drag, or front headlock.

The successful execution of a standup depends on a proper change of levels. But once a wrestler gets to his feet, he should lower his hips (not bend his waist). He thus becomes heavier for the opponent, and it is easier to break his grip and turn to face him.

a

Figure 9.3 Proper technique for changing levels.

b

c

Figure 9.3 *(continued)*

d

Figure 9.3   *(continued)*

Changing Levels Game

BONE FIGHT

Goal

To work on level change and movement

Description

Divide the group into pairs and give each pair a towel. Have each wrestler hold one end of the towel without wrapping it around his hand. Using only one hand, the wrestlers try to break each other's grip on the towel or knock each other off balance. Award a point each time a wrestler breaks his opponent's grip or his opponent's knee touches the mat.

To make the game easier:

⊙ Award a point each time any part of the opponent other than his feet touches the floor.

To make the game harder:

⊙ Shorten the towel.

FACE-OFF

Goal

To learn the hip movement from the bottom position

Description

The bottom wrestler kneels with hands on the mat at his sides. The top wrestler kneels behind the bottom wrestler and underhooks both arms from behind. The bottom person must battle away from the arms and face the top person. The top person must drive the bottom person to his belly and hold him there. The top person cannot lock hands.

To make the game harder:

⊙ The bottom man must start in regular top/bottom position.

FLOPPING FISH

Goal

To learn ways to pin a defender for the fall

Description

Two wrestlers lie flat on their backs side by side (head to head, feet to feet). Each wrestler has his arms and hands flat to the mat and legs straight. To start the "flopping fish," each wrestler will bridge and try to catch the other person on his back.

Score one point for a takedown in which the defender gets to his belly, two points when a fish holds the other to his back for 5 seconds, and three points when a wrestler holds his opponent to his back for 10 seconds. If one wrestler is more skilled than the other, give the less-skilled wrestler more advantages, such as allowing him to start with legs bent or his inside arm across the defender's chest.

CRICKETS AND WICKETS

Goal

To initiate proper level change

Description

Wrestlers work in pairs. One wrestler shoots through a stationary partner's legs (the wicket). Then the shooter leaps back over the partner in a leapfrog motion.

Skill 4: Penetration

To move an opponent from a position of stability (a good stance) and to reduce his potential power (mobility), the wrestler eventually must make contact with and control his opponent's hips. To do so requires that any movement in his direction not be just *to* him, but literally *through* him!

This forward motion through him should be directed toward his hips or the location where his hips will be at a given instant. A line on the mat from the attacking wrestler to his opponent would run directly to his hips (through his legs) and to a point at least 3 feet beyond. We are talking about driving the hips through the opponent's hips. See figure 9.4a–d.

When incorporated into a double-leg tackle, deep penetration will put the wrestler completely through his opponent before the opponent can react. It is important to remember that the step should not only be deep but also directed to the opponent's hips. The secret is not in stepping to where he was, but in anticipating where he's going to be.

a

Figure 9.4   Forward motion to the opponent's hips is essential for good penetration.

b

c

Figure 9.4 *(continued)*

d

Figure 9.4 *(continued)*

Penetration Game

KNEE TAG

Goal

To work on level change and penetration

Description

Divide the group into pairs. Have wrestlers face each other and try to shoot in and tag the inside of their partner's knee. Award a point for each knee touch.

To make the game easier:

○ Have one partner tag and the other defend without using any hands.

To make the game harder:

○ Count only tags to the inside of the knee.

SNEAKY SNAPS

Goal

To practice snapping and moving an opponent with a head tie

Description

One wrestler starts with a head tie. His goal is to be sneaky and attack an opponent with a snapdown instead of a shot or leg attack. The attacker controls the head tie and will circle and move the defender. The defender cannot use his hands for balance or shoot on the attacker. The attacker can either shoot a leg attack and score a takedown for one point or snap his opponent down for two points.

THE WHIZZER

Goal

To control an opponent's motion

Description

Two wrestlers kneel side by side in a 9-foot circle. The whizzer places the inside arm across the opponent's back. The whizzer tries to drive the opponent out of bounds or throw him to his back. The other wrestler does the same. The common mistake for wrestlers is to step over a whizzer, which causes a wrestler to fall to his back.

Skill 5: Lifting

Of all the basic skills, the ability to lift is probably the most important. Too often, however, wrestlers believe that they do not have enough strength. They probably won't if they use only the arms. You see, the strongest muscles in the body are located in the hips and thighs. Although strength is important, the ability to lift depends more on the position of the hips to the opponent than anything else.

Following are the key steps for lifting an opponent (see figure 9.5a–f):

1. Squeeze your opponent to your body with your arms. Do not try to pull him up with the strength of your arms. Simply "secure" him. Regardless of what part of his body you secure, or your position to him (front, back, or side), the two following points apply.

2. Lower your hips into and under his center of gravity (his hips).

3. Lift up with the power in your legs and keep your hips driven into and under him (penetration).

4. Wrestlers have a responsibility when lifting on opponents. The main concept is to return the opponent safely to the mat. Penaltys will occur if this doesn't happen. It is called slamming.

One of the most exciting confrontations in a wrestling match is when two good wrestlers are struggling in an upright position. The wrestler behind tries to keep control of the opponent and get into a position to lift, while the wrestler in front struggles to break the opponent's grasp by lowering his level and extending his arms.

a   *b*

Figure 9.5 Technique for correctly lifting your opponent and safely returning him to the mat.

c

d

Figure 9.5 *(continued)*

e

f

Figure 9.5 *(continued)*

Figure 9.6a–d demonstrates another method of lifting starting from the top and bottom position.

a

b

Figure 9.6   Lifting from the top and bottom position.

c

Figure 9.6 *(continued)*   d

Another interesting matchup occurs when one wrestler gets to the side of the opponent after executing a duck-under but is momentarily stymied. From this position, the wrestler must get the hips down and into the opponent to finish the lift and score.

The lift is also an integral part of the high-crotch takedown. The same principles apply. The arms are used to secure the opponent. The forward thrust of the hips and straightening of the back provide upward momentum, and the lift ensures a successful finish.

Lifting Games

RESCUE MISSION

Goal

To work on lifting

Description

Divide the group into teams of four. Start with three wrestlers on one side of the mat and one on the other. The single wrestler (the rescuer) runs across the mat, lifts one of the teammates, and carries the teammate across the mat. He then runs back and does the same for each of the remaining two teammates. The first team to move all three teammates across the mat scores a point. Alternate rescuers until everyone has had a chance to play that role.

To make the game easier:

⊙ Decrease the distance for the carry or let the rescuer drag the teammates only halfway.

To make the game harder:

⊙ Require teammates to play dead and be limp during the lift and carry.

LOG LIFT

Goal

To learn proper lifting with an emphasis on leg and hip power

Description

Two participants have the same lock on each other. Each locks in reverse lift position around the opponent's body. To get in the lock, each participant must step his right leg to the inside of the other's right leg. Then each leans forward and locks his hands just above the other's waist. On a set mark, each tries to lift the other without tripping the opponent. The goal is to take the opponent off his feet.

STUCK IN THE MUD

Goal

To enhance wrestler's ability to score takedowns and defender's ability to battle against leg attacks

Description

One defender kneels on the left leg, with the right foot on the mat far in front of his knee. The attacker wraps his right arm, armpit deep, above the shoelaces of the kneeling wrestler. On the start, the defending wrestler sits back on the attacker's shoulders. The defender's goal is to keep weight on the attacker and keep him from gaining control of his far leg.

To make the game harder:

⊙ Allow the attacker to stand up with the defender's leg and trip the defender to the mat.

TURK STEP CHASE

Goal

To enhance the wrestler's ability to score back points

Description

The defender is flat on his belly with legs straight. His goal is to crawl to a target, such as out of a circle, by pulling himself along with his elbows and forearms. (Don't let the bottom man crawl with his legs.) The top man prevents his opponent from reaching safety using a turk step. He turns the defender over and secures one of the opponent's legs with both of his own.

Skill 6: Back Step

The back step gets a wrestler into a specific position from which he can lift the opponent. This skill requires the ability to smoothly and quickly rotate the hips into and under the opponent, so that the opponent ends up behind him and over his hips (see figures 9.7a–f and 9.8a–f).

The smooth, quick rotation can be accomplished by bringing the feet close together to create a small point of support, much like that of a child's toy top. From this position, the wrestler can change levels (skill 3), rotate his hips "to and through" the opponent (skill 4), and be in position to lift (skill 5).

The back step can position a wrestler for a headlock and a variety of other maneuvers. Maneuvers involving the back step are distinguished by the part of the opponent's body that is secured. If the head and arm are tied up, it's a headlock; if the hold is over one arm and under the other, it's a hiplock.

a

Figure 9.7 Technique for performing the back step. Note the use of the arm spin in photo d.

b

c

Figure 9.7 *(continued)*

d

e

f

Figure 9.7 *(continued)*

a

b

Figure 9.8 Using the back step to grasp your opponent. Note the use of a headlock in photo c.

c

d

Figure 9.8 *(continued)*

e

f

Figure 9.8 *(continued)*

Back Step Games

SWITCHEROO

Goal

To work on the back step and lifting

Description

Divide the group into pairs. Have partners lock up their arms over and under each other, chest to chest. Without breaking the grip, each wrestler tries to knock the opponent to the ground. The person on top scores a point for each knockdown.

To make the game easier:

⊙ Have the partners lock up only the arms.

To make the game harder:

⊙ Don't allow tripping.

TOE TACKLES

Goal

To initiate takedown attempts using an attacker's legs and feet as tripping instruments

Description

Each wrestler grasps the opponent's shoulders, essentially at arms' length of each other. Neither wrestler can move or pummel for position with his hands, nor can he shoot or snap down the opponent. Points are awarded by using the feet and legs to trip the opponent to the mat to score a takedown. Only successful trips or foot props are scored.

Variation

⊙ To increase the contact, let the wrestlers start chest to chest in an over-under position.

Skill 7: Back Arch

The back arch leads to another very specific position from which to lift. The back arch requires the ability to balance one's own body over a point of support while driving the hips into and under the opponent (skill 4) and going from the feet into a high-arching back bridge. In its ultimate form, it gives rise to the spectacular lifts and throws associated with the international styles. Although some of these throws are not legal under folkstyle and youth rules, the basic arch is found in many of the maneuvers used by top athletes.

The fireman's carry is a perfect example of a move that includes the back arch. The hips are kept in, and the arch is used to throw the opponent to his back. The back arch also is important on all throws, along with the head-outside single-leg, duck-unders, and every maneuver that requires a lift (skill 5). See figure 9.9a–f for techniques of the back arch.

a

Figure 9.9   Performing the back arch to lift and throw your opponent.

b

c   d

Figure 9.9 *(continued)*

e

f

Figure 9.9 *(continued)*

Back Arch Games

SPIDER FIGHT

Goal

To work on the back arch

Description

Divide the group into pairs. Have both wrestlers face away from each other and assume a back bridge, with only hands and feet on the floor. By grabbing, pulling, or pushing their partners, the wrestlers try to knock each other out of the bridge. Award a point for each knockdown.

To make the game easier:

⊙ Have wrestlers use a crab position instead of a spider position.

To make the game harder:

⊙ Allow the wrestlers to use only their left hands to fight.

PUMMELING AROUND

Goal

To increase activity and awareness from a close pummeling situation

Description

Two wrestlers are placed chest to chest in an over-under position, also known as the pummeling position. Young wrestlers often stand straight to get a good feel, so it often helps for them to lean into each other chest to chest. Once in position the two should use control of their underhook and overhook to lift and throw the other to his back. This eventually teaches lateral throws, headlocks, hip tosses, and arm spins.

Putting It All Together

Just because you have taught all Seven Basic Skills effectively, that doesn't mean your wrestlers will always perform them successfully in matches. Their opponents will have more than a little to say about the results of their attempts to apply the skills. However, you need to encourage your wrestlers to develop analytical skills so that they can determine the skill at which they faltered.

For example, if one of your wrestlers attempts the basic single-leg attack and the opponent counters with pressure, your wrestler should know to return immediately to square one. First, he should make certain that he is carrying his body (position) correctly. Then he should move on to skill 2 (lateral, forward, or circular motion) and try to create a new and better angle of attack. Once a good angle is achieved, the wrestler should try changing levels (skill 3) to gain an advantage. Hopefully, by moving through each of the Seven Basic Skills, the wrestler will find the key to lifting and scoring on the opponent.

Learning the sequence of the Seven Basic Skills allows wrestlers to see that all of the many wrestling maneuvers have simple, standard components. This chapter should help you teach your wrestlers these fundamentals. If you do a good job of it, they'll enjoy the sport and probably experience success in their future wrestling matches.

Season Plans

Y ou've learned a lot from this book: what your responsibilities as a coach are, how to communicate well and provide for safety, how to use the games approach to teach and shape skills, and how to coach on match days. But competitions only make up a small portion of your season—you and your athletes will spend more time in practice than in matches. How well you conduct practices and prepare your athletes for competition will greatly affect both you and your athletes' enjoyment and success throughout the season.

In this chapter we present three seasonal plans: one for ages 9 and under, one for ages 10 and 11, and one for ages 12 and over. Use these plans as guidelines for conducting your practices. These plans are not the only way to approach your season, but they do present an appropriate teaching progression. Remember to incorporate the games approach as you use these plans, using Game 1 to put your athletes in a match-like situation that introduces them to the main tactics that you want them to learn that day. Then guide your athletes through a short question-answer session that leads to skill practice. Here you should conduct one or two skill practices in which you will teach athletes the tactic or skill and then conduct a fun drill to reinforce and teach that skill.

Refer to chapter 5 for how to run a practice. In chapter 9 you will find descriptions of the skills and games. Throughout the season plans we refer you to the appropriate pages for the games and skills.

Remember to keep the introductions, demonstrations, and explanations of the tactics and skills brief. As the athletes practice, attend to individual athletes guiding them with tips or with further demonstration. Good luck and good coaching!

Season plans for ages 9 and under

Many children 9 years old and younger have had little or no exposure to wrestling. Don't assume they have any knowledge of the sport. Help them explore the basic tactics and skills, as suggested in the following season plan.

Practice 1

- ⊙ **Purpose:** To learn motion associated with common wrestling situations
- ⊙ **Game:** Bull Riding (see page 108)
- ⊙ **Skill Practice:** Stance (square or stagger), sprawl (downblock and crossblock), hip-heist
- ⊙ **Cool-Down and Review**

Practice 2

- ⊙ **Purpose:** To learn motion in a stance with contact
- ⊙ **Game:** Wrestler's Handshake (see page 103)
- ⊙ **Skill Practice:** Position and motion
- ⊙ **Cool-Down and Review**

Week 2

Practice 3

- ⊙ **Purpose:** To learn basic ways to attack an opponent's hips
- ⊙ **Game:** Bone Fight (see page 112)

- **Skill Practice:** Double leg and single-leg penetration from a high level
- **Cool-Down and Review**

Practice 4

- **Purpose:** To enhance breakdown skills
- **Game:** Bulldozer (see page 104)
- **Skill Practice:** Mat position, changing levels, and balance
- **Cool-Down and Review**

Week 3

Practice 5

- **Purpose:** To learn proper technique in taking an opponent down
- **Game:** Rescue Mission (see page 123)
- **Skill Practice:** Lifting from a double-leg and single-leg position
- **Cool-Down and Review**

Practice 6

- **Purpose:** To practice facing an opponent when out of a good stance while the attacker practices scoring a go-behind.
- **Game:** Spinning Bear (see page 109)
- **Skill Practice:** Motion and level change
- **Cool-Down and Review**

Week 4

Practice 7

- **Purpose:** To learn ways to pin a defender for the fall
- **Game:** Flopping Fish (see page 113)
- **Skill Practice:** Changing levels and motion
- **Cool-Down and Review**

Practice 8

- **Purpose:** To learn hip movement from the bottom
- **Game:** Face-off (see page 113)

⊙ **Skill Practice:** Motion and position
⊙ **Cool-Down and Review**

Week 5

Practice 9

⊙ **Purpose:** To learn ways to reverse control of an opponent
⊙ **Game:** Switchers (see page 103)
⊙ **Skill Practice:** Motion, level change, penetration, lifting
⊙ **Cool-Down and Review**

Practice 10

⊙ **Purpose:** To learn the whizzer as a way to control an opponent's motion
⊙ **Game:** The Whizzer (see page 117)
⊙ **Skill Practice:** Motion, back arch, back step, and level change
⊙ **Cool-Down and Review**

Week 6

Practice 11

⊙ **Purpose:** To learn ways to pin a defender for the fall
⊙ **Game:** Flopping Fish (see page 113)
⊙ **Skill Practice:** Changing levels and motion
⊙ **Cool-Down and Review**

Practice 12

⊙ **Purpose:** To increase awareness of position
⊙ **Game:** Spinning Bear (see page 109)
⊙ **Skill Practice:** Changing levels and motion
⊙ **Cool-Down and Review**

Week 7

Practice 13

⊙ **Purpose:** To increase activity and awareness from a close pum-meling situation

- **Game:** Pummeling Around (see page 135)
- **Skill Practice:** Motion, level change lifting, and back arch
- **Cool-Down and Review**

Practice 14

- **Purpose:** To initiate takedowns using your legs as a tripping or attacking device
- **Game:** Toe Tackles (see page 131)
- **Skill Practice:** Level change, motion, stance, and penetration
- **Cool-Down and Review**

Season Plans for ages 10 and 11

Week 1

Practice 1

- **Purpose:** To learn how to scramble and return to a correct stance
- **Game:** Crack the Whip (see page 109)
- **Skill Practice:** Stance and motion
- **Cool-Down and Review**

Practice 2

- **Purpose:** To learn basic ways to attack an opponent's hips
- **Game:** Knee Tag (see page 116)
- **Skill Practice:** Double leg, single leg, and sweep single
- **Cool-Down and Review**

Week 2

Practice 3

- **Purpose:** To learn to attack an opponent's hips
- **Game:** Bulldozer (see page 104)
- **Skill Practice:** Level change, penetration, stance, and motion
- **Cool-Down and Review**

Practice 4

- ⊙ **Purpose:** To learn hip movement from the bottom
- ⊙ **Game:** Face-off (see page 113)
- ⊙ **Skill Practice:** Motion and position
- ⊙ **Cool-Down and Review**

Week 3

Practice 5

- ⊙ **Purpose:** To increase awareness of position
- ⊙ **Game:** Spinning Bear (see page 109)
- ⊙ **Skill Practice:** Motion and level change
- ⊙ **Cool-Down and Review**

Practice 6

- ⊙ **Purpose:** To learn ways to pin a defender for the fall
- ⊙ **Game:** Flopping Fish (see page 113)
- ⊙ **Skill Practice:** Changing levels and motion
- ⊙ **Cool-Down and Review**

Week 4

Practice 7

- ⊙ **Purpose:** To enhance breakdown skills
- ⊙ **Game:** Bulldozer (Instead of starting from a kneeling position, the down person should start seated with the knees bent to the chest. The goal should be to hip heist or face the bulldozer. The bulldozer, or top-man, should try to break down and flatten the opponent.) (see page 104)
- ⊙ **Skill Practice:** Mat position, changing levels, and balance
- ⊙ **Cool-Down and Review**

Practice 8

- ⊙ **Purpose:** To practice snapping and moving an opponent in a head tie

- **Game:** Sneaky Snaps (see page 117)
- **Skill Practice:** Level change and motion
- **Cool-Down and Review**

Week 5

Practice 9

- **Purpose:** To examine the techniques used in throwing and countering a headlock
- **Game:** Pummeling Around (see page 135)
- **Skill Practice:** Motion, level change lifting and back arch
- **Moves:** Sag headlock for offense and countering techniques for defense
- **Cool-Down and Review**

Practice 10

- **Purpose:** To learn the skill of pummeling, to take an opponent from his feet to his back
- **Game:** Pummeling Around (see page 135)
- **Skill Practice:** Motion, level change lifting and back arch
- **Moves:** Headlock, hip toss, arm throw
- **Cool-Down and Review**

Week 6

Practice 11

Purpose: To understand how to counter a sprawl with the opponent in a front headlock position

- **Game:** Spinning Bear (Perform the Spinning Bear game with one adjustment: The "bear" should give up control of one arm to his opponent to start. The attacker then takes control of his chin and pulls the defender's arm tightly to the opponent's ear by grasping above the elbow.) (see page 109)
- **Skill Practice:** Motion and level change kelly (or hip tip), sucker drag, and backing out safely
- **Cool-Down and Review**

Practice 12

- ⊙ **Purpose:** To learn the whizzer as a way to control the opponent's motion
- ⊙ **Game:** The Whizzer (see page 117)
- ⊙ **Skill Practice:** Motion, level change, penetration, lifting
- ⊙ **Cool-Down and Review**

Week 7

Practice 13

- ⊙ **Purpose:** To learn the skills of taking an opponent to his back from a low-level or front headlock position
- ⊙ **Game:** Tumbling Bear (see page 109)
- ⊙ **Skill Practice:** Motion, level change, position,
- ⊙ **Moves:** Whipover, front quarter-nelson, and cross-face headlock
- ⊙ **Cool-Down and Review**

Practice 14

- ⊙ **Purpose:** To initiate takedowns using your legs as a tripping or attacking device
- ⊙ **Game:** Toe Tackles (see page 131)
- ⊙ **Skill Practice:** Level change, motion, stance, and penetration
- ⊙ **Moves:** Inside trip, foot prop, grapevine
- ⊙ **Cool-Down and Review**

Season Plans for ages 12 and over

Week 1

Practice 1

- ⊙ **Purpose:** To learn motion associated with common wrestling situations
- ⊙ **Game:** Crack the Whip (see page 109)

⊙ **Skill Practice:** Stance (square or stagger), sprawl (downblock and crossblock), and hip heist

⊙ **Cool-Down and Review**

Practice 2

⊙ **Purpose:** To learn basic ways to attack an opponent's hips

⊙ **Game:** Knee Tag (see page 116)

⊙ **Skill Practice:** Double-leg and single-leg sweep

⊙ **Cool-Down and Review**

Week 2

Practice 3

⊙ **Purpose:** To learn advanced ways of taking down an opponent

⊙ **Game:** Bull Riding (see page 108)

⊙ **Skill Practice:** High crotch takedown and fireman's carry

⊙ **Cool-Down and Review**

Practice 4

⊙ **Purpose:** To learn correct starting position for top and bottom

⊙ **Game:** Wrestle from the top and bottom position as described on page 100

⊙ **Skill Practice:** Standup, switch, hip heist, inside stepover. Top man—ankle picks, arm chop with a tight waist, and spiral ride

⊙ **Cool-Down and Review**

Week 3

Practice 5

⊙ **Purpose:** Learn advanced ways of turning an opponent with a leg ride

⊙ **Game:** Bull Riding (see page 108)

⊙ **Skill Practice:** Hipover cross face and power half

⊙ **Cool-Down and Review**

Practice 6

- **Purpose:** To examine the techniques used in throwing and countering a headlock
- **Game:** Pummeling Around (see page 135)
- **Skill Practice:** Sag headlock for offense and countering techniques for defense.
- **Cool-Down and Review**

Week 4

Practice 7

- **Purpose:** To learn advanced ways of taking an opponent to his back from a snapdown
- **Game:** Pummeling Around (see page 135)
- **Skill Practice:** Front headlock whip, front quarter, whipover, and crossface headlock (kaboom)
- **Cool-Down and Review**

Practice 8

- **Purpose:** To learn an advanced way of taking an opponent to his back from the bottom position
- **Game:** Switchers (see page 103)
- **Skill Practice:** Head shrug to a granby cradle
- **Cool-Down and Review**

Week 5

Practice 9

- **Purpose:** To understand how to a counter a sprawl with the opponent in a front headlock, or a front body lock.
- **Game:** Spinning Bear (Adjust to the front headlock and front body lock positions.) (see page 109)
- **Skill Practice:** Back out safely, kelly, sucker drag, and peekout from the high level and low level
- **Cool-Down and Review**

Practice 10

- **Purpose:** To learn an advanced tie-up (the 2 on 1) and the many types of takedowns available from it
- **Game:** Wrestler's Handshake (see page 103)
- **Skill Practice:** Two on one drag, foot prop, double, mule kick, and single
- **Cool-Down and Review**

Week 6

Practice 11

- **Purpose:** To learn basic maneuvers to score from a short sit position
- **Game:** Bulldozer (Instead of starting from a kneeling position, the down person should start seated with the knees bent to the chest. The goal should be to hip heist or face the bulldozer. The bulldozer, or top-man, should try to break down and flatten the opponent.) (see page 104)
- **Skill Practice:** Hip heist, gazonie (or arm wrap), standup, and head shrug
- **Cool-Down and Review**

Practice 12

- **Purpose:** To learn basic ways of moving an opponent from a head tie
- **Game:** Sneaky Snaps (see page 117)
- **Skill Practice:** Snapdowns and shots from a head tie
- **Cool-Down and Review**

Week 7

Practice 13

- **Purpose:** Learn an advanced way of putting a person to his back from both the top position and the neutral position
- **Game:** Turk Step Chase (see page 124)
- **Skill Practice:** Turk step
- **Cool-Down and Review**

Practice 14

⊙ **Purpose:** To learn the skill of pummeling, to take an opponent from his feet to his back

⊙ **Game:** Pummeling Around (see page 135)

⊙ **Skill Practice:** Headlock, hip toss, arm throw, body lock, outside metzger

⊙ **Cool-Down and Review**

Injury Report

Name of athlete _____

Date _____

Time _____

First aider (name) _____

Cause of injury _____

_____

Type of injury _____

Anatomical area involved _____

Extent of injury _____

_____

_____

First aid administered _____

_____

_____

Other treatment administered _____

_____

_____

_____

Referral action _____

_____

_____

_____

_____
First aider (signature)

Emergency Information Card

Athlete's name _____ Age _____

Address _____

Phone _____ S.S.# _____

Sport _____

List two persons to contact in case of emergency:

Parent or guardian's name _____

Address _____

Home phone _____ Work phone _____

Second person's name _____

Address _____

Home phone _____ Work phone _____

Relationship to athlete _____

Insurance co. _____ Policy # _____

Physician's name _____ Phone _____

IMPORTANT

Is your child allergic to any drugs? _____ If so, what? _____

Does your child have any other allergies? (e.g., bee stings, dust) _____

Does your child have ____ asthma, ____ diabetes, or ____ epilepsy?

Is your child on any medication? _____ If so, what? _____

Does your child wear contacts? _____

Is there anything else we should know about your child's health or physical condition? If yes, please explain. _____

_____

_____

_____

_____

_____   _____

Signature   Date

Emergency Response Card

Information for emergency call
(Be prepared to give this information to the EMS dispatcher)

1. Location _____

   Street address _____

   City or town _____

   Directions (cross streets, landmarks, etc.) _____

   _____

   _____

2. Telephone number from which call is being made _____

3. Caller's name _____

4. What happened _____

   _____

   _____

   _____

   _____

   _____

5. How many persons injured _____

6. Condition of victim(s) _____

7. Help (first aid) being given _____

   _____

   _____

   _____

Note: Do not hang up first. Let the EMS dispatcher hang up first.